Reconstructed

1790 CENSUS
of
DELAWARE

By:
Leon DeValinger, Jr.

Southern Historical Press, Inc.
Greenville, South Carolina

This volume was reproduced
from a personal copy located in
the Publishers private library

Please direct all correspondence and book orders to:
SOUTHERN HISTORICAL PRESS, Inc.
PO Box 1267
Greenville, SC   29602-1267

Originally printed 1954
ISBN #978-1-63914-307-8
Printed in the United States of America

RECONSTRUCTED 1790 CENSUS OF DELAWARE

By LEON deVALINGER, JR., *State Archivist*, Dover, Delaware

Shortly after the adoption of the Federal Constitution in 1789 (Delaware had become the first state in the Union by unanimously ratifying on December 7, 1787), the new Congress, realizing the great need of a census to properly evaluate the Nation, passed an act, approved March 1, 1790, which provided for the enumeration of the inhabitants of the United States. The act required the marshals of the judicial districts of the then states of Maine, New Hampshire, Massachusetts, Connecticut, New York, New Jersey, Pennsylvania, Delaware, Maryland, Virginia, Kentucky, North Carolina, South Carolina, and Georgia to enumerate the inhabitants in their respective districts.[1] The marshals and their appointed assistants were to list their findings in a schedule under the six headings: "Names of heads of families; Free white males of 16 years and upwards, including heads of families; Free white males under 16 years; Free white females, including heads of families; All other free persons; Slaves."[2] In addition, the act provided that Indians not taxed were to be omitted from the census and the marshals were to distinguish free persons (including those bound to service for a term of years), and the sex and color of free persons. Nine months were allowed for this then prodigiously difficult job, considering the many remote rural areas and the great hardships of traveling.

The National Archives has obtained from the Bureau of the Census the original schedules which were returned originally to the President and later to the Secretary of State.[3] Unfortunately there are no census returns for the States of Delaware, Georgia, Kentucky, New Jersey, Tennessee, and Virginia.[4] It is generally believed that these records are not on file because they were destroyed when the British burned the Capitol on August 24, 1814, during the War of 1812. There is, however, the possibility that these census schedules may have been lost before they ever came to Washington. This thought was suggested to the writer by a former employee[5] of the Bureau who pointed out that a resolution of Congress, approved May 28, 1830, provided:

> . . . That the clerks of the several District and Supreme Courts of the United States be and they are hereby directed to transmit to the Secretary of State the several returns of the enumeration of the inhabitants of the United States filed in their respective offices by direction of the several acts of Congress, passed the first of March, one thousand seven hundred and ninety; the twenty eighth of February one thousand eight hundred; the twenty sixth of March one thousand eight hundred and ten; and the fourteenth of March one thousand eight hundred and twenty.[6]

This resolution clearly implies that by 1830 the returns for the first four census enumerations had not been sent to Washington and were in the custody of officials in the judicial districts of the states.

On October 27, 1791, President Washington transmitted to Congress a summary of the returns of the First Census. This, now rare, publication disloses the following interesting statistics for Delaware:

---

[1] Heads of Families First Census of the United States: 1790 Maryland, compiled by Bureau of the Census, Washington, D. C., 1907, page 6.

[2] Idem.

[3] Ibid. page 4.

[4] Ibid, page 3.

[5] Miss Mary C. Oursler, Washington, D. C.

[6] Register of Debates in Congress 1830, 21st Congress 1st Session, page 50 Appendix to Gales-Seaton's Register.

Free white males 16 yrs. and upward	Free white males under 16 yrs.	Free white females	All other free persons	Slaves	Total[7]
11,783	12,143	22,384	3,899	8,887	59,096

Delaware's population at this time was the smallest in the Nation, but there was not such a great disparity between it and the 68,825 of Rhode Island, the 73,677 of Kentucky, or the 82,548 of Georgia. The following table is included to supply population statistics on a county basis from the foregoing summary of 1790:[8]

sought in the first census. Likewise, names of those who were not property owners are missing as also are enumerations of women, children, or slaves. Although this reconstructed census will not be as complete as the original would have been, it is hoped that the results of long

COUNTIES	WHITE			COLORED		AGGREGATE
	MALE	FEMALE	TOTAL	FREE	SLAVES	
New Castle _____	8,720	7,767	16,487	639	2,562	19,688
Kent _____	7,172	6,878	14,050	2,570	2,300	18,920
Sussex _____	8,034	7,739	15,773	690	4,025	20,488
Total _____	23,926	22,384	46,310	3,899	8,887	59,096

Genealogists, research workers, and historians working in the records of Delaware have long been inconvenienced by the loss of the 1790 census records. It was to remedy this situation that some years ago the writer undertook to reconstruct the first census from the tax lists of the State. This type of record was selected, rather than other records, as its contents resemble those of the census returns. These tax lists contain the name of the taxable or head of family. It is true that they fail to give the other data

hours of compilation and transcribing will be beneficial. It should also be explained that the reconstructed census is arranged by counties beginning with New Castle, followed by Kent and Sussex. These counties are further arranged by Hundreds, a political subdivision, peculiar to Delaware. The Hundreds are arranged alphabetically and the names are listed in the same manner under each Hundred. Where a tax list for the year 1790 was not extant the list for the year closest to that date was selected. In each instance the compiler has retained the original spelling of the assessment lists and has added only an apostrophe to the names of estates for clarity or placed in brackets the usual spelling of a name for easier identification.

[7]Heads of Families First Census . . . , op. cit. page 8.

[8]Atlas of the State of Delaware, by D. G. Beers, pub. by Pomeroy & Beers, Philadelphia, Penna., 1868.

NEW CASTLE COUNTY
APPOQUINIMINK HUNDRED

Alle, Jeremiah
Allen, Abraham
Allen, John
Allfree, John
Allfree, Lewis
Allfree, William, Esq.
Allfree, William, Jr.
Allman, Isaac, Estate
Alrich, Joseph
Alrich, Wessel, Estate
Alritch [Alrich], Harmanus, Estate
Alston, Arther, Estate
Alston, John
Anderson, Abraham
Anderson, Andrew
Anderson, Jacob
Anderson, John
Andrews, John
Appelton, John
Appelton, Robert, Estate
Appleton, Thomas
Ash, Joseph, Estate
Atkinson, James
Atkinson, Sampson

Ballard, Jonathan
Barlow, John
Barlow, Josiah
Barlow, Nicholas
Barlow, Simon
Bassett, Elias
Bassett, John
Bassett, Joseph, Estate
Bassett, Nathaniel
Beadley, Elizabeth
Beard, Duncan
Beard, John
Beards, Alexander, Estate
Beaston, Jeremiah
Beck, John
Belveal, Cornelius
Bennett, Ebenezer
Bennett, Perry
Bennett, Thomas
Biggs, Jonathan
Biggs, Levi, Estate
Bilderback, Joseph, Estate
Bodyst, John
Bostick, Joseph
Bostick, Nathan
Bostick, Samuel
Bouchell, Sluytor, Dr.

Bowman, Charles
Bowman, Peter
Bowyer, Abraham
Bowyer, Nathaniel, Estate
Bowyer, Thomas, Estate
Bradford, William
Brown, Allen
Brown, Edmond, Estate
Brown, George
Brown, John
Brown, Thomas, Estate
Bryan, Thomas
Buchanan, James
Buckson, James
Budd, Thomas, Estate
Budd, William
Bullock, Timothy
Burch, Christopher
Burch, George
Burch, Joseph
Burcham, Abraham
Burkelow, John
Burnett, Andrew
Byard's [Bayard], Peter, Estate

Callahan, John
Cantwell, Richard, Esq., Estate
Cartwright, Abraham
Cartwright, Jacob
Cartwright, Jacob, Jr.
Carvell, John
Caulk, Benjamin
Caulk, Jacob, and Estate
Caulk, Rachel, Estate
Chambers, James
Chance, Alexander, Estate
Chance, Edmond
Chandler, Samuel
Clark, John
Clark, William, Esq., Estate
Clayton, Isaac
Clayton, Jacob
Clayton, John
Clayton, Joseph
Clemmins, John
Cohe, William
Cole, Isaac
Cole, Perry
Colgate, Bridget, Estate
Collins, John
Conner, John
Coombs, William

Corbit, Daniel, Estate
Corbit, Israel, Estate
Corbit, William, Estate
Cornwell, William
Cox, Thomas
Crady, Martin, Estate
Crawford, John, Esq.
Crodick's, Richard, Estate
Crouch, Benjamin
Crouch, John
Cruzen, Garret
Cruzen, Jacob
Cruzen, Peter
Culley, William
Cummins, Daniel, Estate
Cummins, Samuel
Cummins, Timothy, Estate
Currey, Charles
Curry, Jesse

David, David
David, Eleazer
David, Thomas
Davis, Lewis
Davis, William
Davy, James
Dawson, Isaac
Deakyne, George
Deakyne, Jacob
Deakyne, John
Deakyne, Joseph, Estate
Delany, Denis, Estate
Denney, William, Estate
Dickinson, Joseph
Dickinson, Philemon
Doney, Isaac, Estate
Donnelly, Michael
Dorrel, Daniel
Dorrel, Jeremiah
Durham, Mathew
Durrah, John, Estate
Dushane, Garret, Estate

Ecord, Andrew
Edwards, Andrew, Estate
Edwards, Edmond
Elliott, Alexander, Estate
Elliott, James
Emmory, Gideon
Empson, Thomas, Estate
Everitt, Abraham
Everitt, Charles
Everitt, Charles, Jr.
Everitt, William

Fields, Abraham
Fields, Allen
Fields, William, Estate
Fips, George
Fips, William
Fisher, Fenwick, Estate
Fitzgerald, James
Fitzgerald, Thomas, Estate
Fols, Frederick
Fortner, Nathaniel, Estate
Fowler, Benjamin
Fowler, William
Francis, John
Frazer, William, Estate
French, Babel

Gallaway, John
George, Joshua, Estate
George, Sidney, Estate
Gibbens, Stephen
Gibbs, Isaac, Estate
Giffee, David
Giffee, John
Ginn, Moses
Ginn, William
Gooding, John, Estate
Gooding, William
Green, Jacob
Greenwood, William, Estate
Griffen, David, Estate
Griffen, Ebenezer
Griffen, Mathew
Griffen, Samuel
Griffen's, William, Estate
Griffeth, Richard, Estate
Grindage, William, Estate
Gyles, Joshua

Hackett, Abraham
Hackett, Andrew
Hackett, Joseph
Hall, John
Hamman, Nicholas, Estate
Hamon, John
Hannah, Archibald
Hanson, Nicholas
Hardin, Edmond, Estate
Harman, Abraham, Estate
Harris, Jacob
Harris, James
Harris, Joseph, Estate
Hart, Garret, Estate
Hart, James
Hart, William

APPOQUINIMINK HUNDRED (Continued)

Hartup, Thomas
Harwood, John, Estate
Haughey, James, Estate
Haughey, Marinas
Hawkens, John
Hawkens, Samuel
Hawks, Joseph
Hazell, James
Heath, Charles
Heath, Daniel C.
Henry, James
Hollett, Benjamin
Hollett, Richard
Holliday, Benjamin
Holliday, Joseph, Estate
Holliday, Thomas
Hood, John
Hood, Robert
Howell, Evin
Howell, John
Huett, Henry
Huff, Jonathan
Hunt, Charles
Hurlock, John
Hurlock, William
Hutchison, Joseph
Hyatt, Isaac
Hyatt, James

Johns, Benjamin
Johns, Jehu
Johns, John, Estate
Johnson. Benjamin
Johnson, Jacob
Johnson, John
Johnson, Robert
Johnson, William
Johnson, William, Jr.
Jones, Griffeth
Jones, John, Esq., Estate
Jones, Richard
Jones, Solomon
Jones, Thomas
Jordan, William, Estate

Kanady, David, Estate
Kane, Francis
Keas, Richard, Estate
King, Cornelus, Estate
King, Jacob, Estate
King, John
Knotts, Edward

Latheram, James
Latomur [Latimer], James, Estate
Laughlin, Robert

Leonard, Henry
Lewis, Jehu, Estate
Liston, Abraham, Estate
Liston, John
Liston, William, Estate
Litman, Abraham
Litman, Henry
Litman, Isaac
Lloyd, Edward, Estate
Lockerman, Benjamin
Lockerman, John, Estate
Lockhart, Andrew
Lubey, Patrick
Luper, James
Lyle, James
Lyons, Patrick, Estate

McBride, Benjamin
McCloud, Alexander, Estate
McComb's, Eleazer, Estate
McDonald, Jeremiah
McFarling, Alexander
McKean, Thomas, Estate
McKean, William, Estate
McKeay, Leonard, Estate
McLane, William
McMurphy, Archabald
McMurphy, Robert, Estate
McVay, Owen
McWilliams, Richard, Estate
Mannon, Benjamin
Marcer, William
Marr, Thomas
Marsh, Truax
Marshall, Moses, Estate
Marsilley, John
Martin, David
Martin, Edward
Martin, George
Martin, James, Estate
Martin, John, Estate
Martin, William, Estate
Mathews, Hugh, Estate
Maulster, Benjamin
Maulster, John
Merritt, Benjamin, and Estate
Mills, Alexander, Estate
Mitchell, Charles
Moffett, George, Estate
Moffett, Haley
Moor, Charles
Moor, James
Moor, John
Moore, James, Jr.
Mullen, Lasly

Nash, James, Estate
Nash, Jesse
Nash, John
Naudain, Arnold
Naudain, Arnold, Jr.
Naudain, Cornelius
Naudain, Cornelus, Jr.
Naudain, Elias
Naudain, Elias, Jr.
Naudain, Larrox
Noxon, Benjamin, Estate

Offley, Michael
O'hara, Henry, Estate

Parker, John, Estate
Pearce, Henry
Pearce, Henry W., Estate
Pearson, Aaron
Pearson, Abraham
Pearson, John
Pearson, Richard
Pearson, Richard, Jr.
Pearson, William
Peckard, Henry, Estate
Peckard, Peter
Pennington, Abraham
Pennington, Daniel
Pennington, Isaac
Pennington, Jacob
Peterson, James
Pollard, William, and Estate
Pope, Charles, Estate
Power, James
Preston, Jonas
Price, John, Estate
Pryor, John
Pryor, John, Jr.
Pryor, William
Pugh, Jacob, Estate

Rahow, Paul
Ratliff, Isaac
Ratliff, John
Read, John
Read, Thomas
Reading, Philip, Estate
Redman, David, Estate
Reynold, George
Reynold, Jacob
Reynold, James, Estate
Reynold, Nicholas
Reynold, Richard
Reynold, William
Reynolds, John

Richardson, Benjamin
Richardson, John, Estate
Richardson, William
Robb, Jehu
Robb, Jessee
Roberts, Edward
Rogers, William, Estate
Rothwell, Abraham, Estate
Rothwell, Jared
Rothwell, Thomas
Rothwell, William
Ryall, Jacob
Rye, John, Estate
Ryland, Alrich
Ryland, Stephen

Saunders, Joseph
Savin, John
Schee, Cornelus
Schee, Hannah, Estate
Schee, Harmanus, Estate
Schee, James
Scott, John, Estate
Scott, Samuel
See, Isaac
See, Richard
Shaw, James
Shawn, Joseph
Simons, Thomas
Simpson, Isaac
Skillinton, Thomas
Smith, Charles
Smith, James
Smith, Joseph, Estate
Smith, William
Snell, Jacob
Staats, Abraham, Estate
Staats, David
Staats, Ephraim, Estate
Staats, Garrett
Staats, George
Staats, Isaac, Estate
Staats, Isaac, Jr.
Staats, Jacob, Estate
Staats, Jacob, Sr., Estate
Standish, Miles
Stanford, Joseph
Stanley, Benjamin, Estate
Stanley, John
Stanley, Robert
Stanley, Robert, Jr.
Sterling, Abraham
Sterling, James
Sturges, John
Sutton, Ashberry

Taylor, Abraham
Taylor, Abraham, Jr.
Taylor, John
Taylor, Richard, weaver
Taylor, Richard, Estate
Test, Thomas
Tharp, Thomas
Thomas, Isaac
Townsend, John, Estate
Truax, James
Turner, James
Turner, John Estate
Tush, Jacob
Tybout, Andrews, Estate

Upton, Obediah

Vanbebber, Henry, Estate
Vandegrift, Ebenezer
Vandyke, Benjamin
Vandyke, Jacob
Vanhorn, Barnet
Vanhorn, Paul
Vansandt, Nehemiah

Walker, John
Walker, Nicholas
Walraven, Elias
Walraven, William
Ward, George
Ward, George, Jr.
Ward, Joseph
Watts, Joseph, Estate
Weaver, Christopher
Webb, Hollen

Webster, Evin T.
Weldon, Abraham
Weldon, Isaac
Weldon, James, Estate
Weldon, John, Estate
Weldon, Joseph, Estate
Weldon, Routh
Weldon, William
Whitall, William
White, Robert
Wiggins, Charles
Wiggins, Mathew
Wiles, John
Wiles, Robert, Estate
Wilkinson, Bayman
Williams, Abraham, Estate
Williams, Benjaman
Williams, Cornelus
Williams, Derrick
Williams, Elijah
Williams, William
Wilmore, James, Estate
Wilmore, William, Estate
Wilson, David, Estate
Woodell, William
Wooderson, William
Woodkeeper, Jacob
Woodkeeper, William
Worknot's, Alexander, Estate
Wright, George
Wright, John
Wright, William
Wynkoop, Abraham, Estate
Wynkoop, James, Estate

BRANDYWINE HUNDRED

Afforn, Robert
Allman, John
Anderson, William
Askew, John
Askew, Parker

Babb, Thom[as]
Backhous, Jacob
Baker, Peter
Baldwin, Eli, Estate
Batton, George
Batton, Thom[as]
Beason, Jonathan
Bedford, Gunning, Estate
Beeson, David
Beeson, Edward, Estate
Beeson, Jasper
Beeson, Thom[as]

Bell, John
Bemster, James
Bird, John, Estate
Bird, Thom[as]
Bonsil, Phillip
Boss, Henery
Bradford, John
Bratton, Jacob
Bratton, Robert
Brown, Daniel
Brown, John
Bufington, Joseph
Bush, John

Cable, Daniel
Can, James
Carpindor, Sam[uel]

Cartmill, George
Cartmill, Thom[as], Jr.
Cartmill, Thom[as], Sr.
Cellum, John, Estate
Chandler, Amor
Chandler, Ann, Estate
Chandler, John
Claiton, John
Cloud, Joseph
Cloud, Nathaniel
Cloud, Robert
Cloud, W[illia]m
Cobern, Jacob
Collet, James, Estate
Council, John
Curts, John

Davis, Andrew
Davis, Edward
Davis, Elijah
Davis, George
Davis, Isaac
Davis, Joseph
Day, Francis
Day, Joseph
Derrickson, Cornelius, Jr.
Derrickson, Cornelius, Sr.
Derrickson, W[illia]m, Estate
Derrixson, Alen
Dick, Alex[ander], Estate
Dick, Jacob
Dickingson, John, Estate
Dixon, John, Estate
Dodd, Alax[ander]
Dun, Henry
Dutton, Jacob
Dutton, Joseph

Ellet, Joseph, Estate
Elliott, Benjamin
Elliott, Mark, Jr., Estate
Elliott, Mark, Sr., Estate
Elliott, William, Jr.
Ellit, John
Ellotts, John
Ellott, William
Enok, John
Enos, Francis

File, John
Fillips [Phillips], Thom[as]
Folks, John
Ford, Abraham, Estate
Ford, Benjamin
Ford, David

Ford, James
Ford, Philip
Ford, Thom[as]
Ford, W[illia]m, Estate
Ford, W[illia]m, Sr.
Forwood, William
Foulk, W[illia]m, Estate
Frorwood, Jehu

Gest, Abraham
Gibson, Andrew
Gibson, Thom[as], Estate
Giest, Sam[ue]l
Gilpin, Ann, Estate
Gilpin, Tho[ma]s, Estate
Gilpin, Vinson, Estate
Gorby, Joseph
Grub, James
Grub, Peter
Grubb, Adam, Estate
Grubb, Amor
Grubb, Benjamin
Grubb, Emanuel
Grubb, Isaac
Grubb, John
Guest, Henry

Hamilton, James
Handby, Richard
Hart, Denis
Hayburn, George
Hedge, Joseph, Estate
Hews, Levy [Hughs]
Hickling, William
Hisar, John
Hooton, Elijah
Hunter, John
Husbands, John
Husbands, W[illia]m
Hustin, James
Huston, David
Huston, John
Hysar, Gidion

Jackson, Joseph, Jr.
Jackson, Joseph, Sr.
James, John, Esq.
Jarvus, John
Jeffris, James
Jestison, Richard
Johnson, Abraham
Johnson, Simon, Estate
Jones, Isaac, Estate
Jones, Thom[as]
Jordan, Alax[ander]

BRANDYWINE HUNDRED (Continued)

Kain, Thom[as], Esq.
Kaneyday, John
Kellam, Richard
Kelly, Neenl [Neal]
Kennedy, Nathaniel
Ketlan, Moses
Killpatrick, Daniel
Kilwell, George
Kirk, Caleb, Estate

Lambert, Zacheriah
Landers, George, Estate
Landers, Sam[uel]
Lea, John, Estate
Lea, Thom[as]
Lewis, Abram
Little, Henery
Little, W[illia]m
Littler, Robart, Estate
Lodgse, Sam[ue]l, Sr.
Loge, Sam[ue]l, Jr.
Long, David
Long, John
Long, W[illia]m

McBride, Daniel
McBride, Sam[uel], Estate
McClen, Joshua
McClintock, James
McClintock, Samuel
McClintock, Thom[as]
McClintock, W[illia]m
McCloud, W[illia]m
McClosky, Patrick
McClure, W[illia]m
McDonald, W[illia]m
McGlauchlin, John
McGlocughlin, W[illia]m
McKee, Andrew
McKee, Andrew, Jr.
McKee, James
McKee, John
McKee, W[illia]m
McKeever, Isaac
McKim, Thom[as], Estate

Marshall, Sam[ue]l, Estate
Marshall, Joseph, Estate
Martin, George
Mayson, W[illia]m
Millar, Phillip
Milmen, Nathan, Estate
Mingle, Frederick

Moffet, Robert
Moore, Richard
Moore, W[illia]m
More, Francis
Morris, Robert, Estate
Mortanson, Joshua
Mortinson, Mark
Morton, John, Estate
Morton, Robert, Estate
Mortonson, Ann, Estate
Mosely, George
Murphy, James
Myars, Henery, Estate

Newlin, Cyros
Nickholls, George
Nicholls, John
Nixon, George
Nixon, James
Nuland, Thom[as]

Oldmond, Thom[as]
Ore, Robert
Owns, Sam[ue]l

Pamba, Isarel
Parker, W[illia]m
Peirce, John (son of Jose)
Peirce, Sam[ue]l
Peirce, Timothy, Sr.
Pennal, Nathan, Estate
Penney, Arther
Perkins, Caleb
Perkins, Thom[as]
Peters, Rechard, Estate
Peterson, Israel
Peterson, Lufloff
Pierce, Amor
Pierce, Benjamin
Pierce, George
Pierce, Henery, and Estate
Pierce, John, Jr.
Pierce, John, Sr.
Pierce, Joseph
Pierce, Levy
Pierce, Robert, Estate
Pilligan, W[illia]m
Pirce, Timothy (Rich's son)
Pirce, Timothy, Jr.
Plunke, James
Polson, George
Preston, James
Price, John, Estate

Price, Richard
Prichard, John, Estate
Prince, Adam
Prince, John
Pyke, Ham[ilton]
Pyke, Jacob
Pyke, W[illia]m
Pyle, Robert, Estate

Ranals, Richard
Ray, John
Reed, Elias, Estate
Reed, W[illia]m
Reynolds, John
Rice, Robert
Rice, W[illia]m
Roberdson, Thom[as] (Jam's. son)
Robinson, Abraham, Estate
Robinson, Charles
Robinson, George, and Estate
Robinson, John
Robinson, Tho[mas], Esq.
Robinson, Valintin
Robonson, Thom[as], Jr.
Rynold, Benjamin

Sail [Seal], Caleb, Estate
Shallcross, Joseph, Estate
Shanks, W[illia]m
Sharpley, Daniel, Estate
Sharpley, George
Sharpley, William
Shaw, Archabald
Shelley, James
Sinix, Seneca
Sinnix, Henery
Smith, Jacob
Smith, James (taylor)
Smith, John
Smith, Joseph
Smith, Robert
Smith, Thom[as], Jr.
Smith, Thom[as], Sr.
Smith, Thomas, Estate
Smith, W[illia]m
Smith, William, Sr.
Smithel, Joseph
Soott, John
Star, Isaac, Estate
Star, W[illia]m, Estate
Stedham, Henery, and Estate
Stedham, Jacob
Stedham, Jonas, Estate

Stevenson, Jacob
Stevenson, W[illia]m
Stevinson, James
Stewart, James
Stewart, Samuel
Stilley, John, Estate
Syvel, James

Talley, David
Talley, Edward
Talley, John
Talley, Sam[ue]l
Talley, Thom[as], Sr.
Talley, W[illia]m, Jr.
Talley, W[illia]m, Sr.
Tally, Elihu
Tally, Joseph
Tally, Thom[as], Jr.
Tatnall, Joseph
Taylor, George, Estate
Taylor, Joseph
Thomas, Joseph, Estate
Thompson, Hugh, Estate
Tussey, W[illia]m

Vandever, John, Jr.
Vandiveer, W[illia]m
Vandiver, John, Sr.
Vandver, Peter
Veneman, W[illia]m, Estate
Verts, Frederick

Walker, John
Wallace, James
Webster, Henery
Webster, Thom[as]
Weer, Joseph
Weldon, Eli
Weldon, Jacob
Welsh, John
Welsh, Margit, Estate
White, George, Estate
White, Peter
Williamson, Adam, Estate
Wills, Jerim'ah
Wilson, George, Estate
Wilson, James
Wilson, William, Estate
Withrow, John
Wolbough, Peter, Estate
Wood, W[illia]m
Worral, Benjamin, Estate
Wrighter, George

CHRISTIANA HUNDRED

Abbot, John
Abraham, Isaac
Ackroyd, John, Estate
Adams, Daniel Y.
Adams, James
Adams, James, Jr.
Adams, John
Aiken, W[illia]m, Estate
Alderdice, Abrah[a]m
Alexander, George
Alexander, James
Alexander, John
Allison, Margaret, Estate
Allison, Sarah, Estate
Alrich, Benj[amin], Estate
Alrich, Su[s]an[n]a, Estate
Alrichs, Jonas
Amors, Tho[ma]s
Anderson, Art[hu]r
Anderson, Charles
Anderson, George
Anderson, Jacob
Anderson, Jacob, Jr.
Anderson, John
Anderson, Josiah
Anderson, Sam[uel]
Andrews, Isaac
Andrews, Sam[uel]
Andrews, Sarah, Estate
Armor, W[illia]m
Armstrong, Ann, Estate
Armstrong, Archib[a]ld
Armstrong, John, Estate
Armstrong, John, Jr.
Armstrong, Rob[er]t
Armstrong, William
Arnold, William
Ashburnham, Joseph
Ashby, W[illia]m
Ashton, William
Augusta, David
Augusta, John
Aull, John

Backhouse, Strainge
Bail, John
Bail, Margaret, Estate
Bailey, Joseph
Baldwin, John
Baldwin, Joseph
Baldwin, Levi
Baldwin, W[illia]m, Estate
Ball, William, Estate

Bancroft. . . ., Doctor
Barber, John
Barber, W[illia]m
Barker, Sam[uel], Estate
Barnard, John
Barnes, Ja[me]s
Barnett, Charles
Barnett, Jacob
Barnett, Samson
Barry, Henry
Bartram, John, Estate
Bayard, James A., Esq.
Bean, Elish
Bean, Eliza
Beatty, John
Bedford, Gunning, Esq.
Beeson, Tho[ma]s
Bell, James
Bennett, Amos
Bennett, Joseph
Benson, John
Bentley, Baz[i]l
Best, Henry
Betson, John
Bigham, Hugh
Bingham, John
Black, James
Blackford, Garard, Jr.
Blackford, Garrett, Sr.
Blackford, John
Bonsall, Phillip, Estate
Bonsall, Vinc[en]t
Boon, James
Booth, Ja[me]s
Bowles, John
Bowles, Tho[ma]s
Bowman, John
Bowman, Paul
Boyd, Matthew
Boyd, Robert
Braden, James, Jr.
Braden, James, Sr.
Bradfield, Edward
Bradford, Sam[ue]l
Bradford, W[illia]m
Bratton, Robert, Estate
Briggs, John
Brindley, James
Brinton, David
Brobson, James
Brooks, John, Estate
Brooks, Tho[ma]s
Broom, Jacob, Esq.

Broom, James
Broom, Natheon
Brown, Abraham
Brown, Dan[ie]l
Brown, Elisha
Brown, Israel
Brown, Nathanel
Brown, Rob[er]t
Bryan, James
Bryan, John
Brynberg, John
Brynberg, Peter
Brynberg, Swithen
Bryson, Barney
Bryson, John
Buckingham, James
Bumbiggar, Jacob
Burrett, Benj[amin]
Bush, David, Jr.
Bush, George
Bush, John, Estate
Bush, Sam[uel]
Byars, James
Byars, Sam[uel]
Byrnes, Dan[iel], Estate
Byrnes, Sam[uel]

Caldwell, John, Estate
Caldwell, Thomas
Campbell, George
Campbell, James
Campbell, Samuel
Canady, Nath[anie]l
Canby, Benj[ami]n
Canby, Jonas
Canby, Sam[uel]
Canby, Tho[ma]s
Canby, William
Capelle, [Joseph], Doctor
Carmet, Owen
Carney, Peter, Estate
Carney, Tho[ma]s, Estate
Carson, John, Estate
Carson, Richard, Estate
Carter, Charles
Casho, Jacob
Cask, Edw[ar]d
Casky, Robert
Casky, Sam[ue]l
Catherwood, And[re]w
Catherwood, Charles
Celso, John
Chambers, John
Chandler, Ann, Estate
Chandler, Benj[amin], Estate

Chandler, Caleb, Estate
Chandler, Christ[opher]
Chandler, David, B. smith
Chandler, George
Chandler, Isaac
Chandler, Jesse, Estate
Chandler, John, Estate
Chandler, Joseph
Chandler, Thomas
Charley, Sam[uel]
Clark, David
Clark, George
Clark, Hugh
Clark, John, hatter
Clark, Tho[ma]s, Jr.
Clark, W[illia]m
Clayton, Jacob
Cleancy, William
Cling, Jacob
Cloud, Dan[ie]l
Cloud, Harlin
Cloud, John
Clyne, Jacob
Cobner, Martha, Estate
Cochran, Dan[ie]l, Estate
Cockshott, John
Coile, Mike
Collins, Barny
Collins, John
Collins, Nichol
Collins, Stephen, Estate
Colsberry, And[re]w·
Colsberry, Henry
Colter, John
Commons, Joseph
Cooch, Tho[ma]s, Estate
Cooke, Benj[amin]
Cooke, William
Coram, Robert
Cox, Moses
Cox, Tho[ma]s
Craig, Fred[eric]k
Craig, Tho[ma]s
Craige, William
Crampton, John
Crampton, Nath[a]n
Crawford, Isaac
Crawford, John
Creery, William
Crips, And[re]w
Crips, Cornel[iu]s
Crips, Jonas
Crips, Matthew
Crosby, Joseph
Crosby, Patrick

Crossan, John
Crow, George, Estate
Crow, Thomas
Croxin, Archib[a]ld
Crozer, W[illia]m
Cummings, W[illia]m, Estate

Davidson, Al[e]x[ande]r, Jr.
Davidson, David
Davidson, Hez[e]k[ia]h, Estate
Davidson, John
Davis, Peter
Davis, Thomas
Daws, Jonathan. Estate
Daws, Rumford, Estate
Dawson, John
Dean, Joseph, Estate
Dean, Sam[uel]
Dehaven, Edward
Delaplain, James
Delaplain, Sam[uel]
Dempsey, William
Derrickson, Cornel[iu]s
Derrickson, David
Derrickson, Jacob
Derrickson, Joseph
Derrickson, William
Derrickson, Zach[a]r[ia]h
Dickey, Archib[a]ld
Dickinson, John, Esq.
Dilworth, George, Estate
Dingee, Jacob, Estate
Dingee, Obad[ia]h
Dirrickson, Peter
Dixon, Dan[iel]
Dixson, Isaac
Dixson, John, Estate
Dixson, Sam[uel], Estate
Dixson, Thomas
Dixson, W[illia]m
Donaldson, David
Donaldson, James
Dowdle, Eliz[abet]h, Estate
Dowlan, John
Duff, Thomas, Esq.
Dulap, John
Dulaplain, Nehemiah
Duncan, Patr[ic]k
Dushane, Corn[e]l[iu]s
Dutton, Fr[a]n[c]as

Eccles, Rob[er]t, Estate
Elliott, William
Entrican, George, Estate

Erwin, John
Erwin, Sam[uel]
Evans Charles
Evans, Evan
Evans, John
Evans, Jonathan
Evans, Joseph
Evans, Olifer
Evans, Theop[hi]l[u]s

Farson, Jean, Estate
Fauss, Nichols, Estate
Ferriss, John
Ferriss, Zach[a]r[ia]h
Ferriss, Ziba
File, Jos[eph]
Finister, Alex[ande]r
Finley, Charles
Fisher & Gilpin Estate
Fisher, James
Flemming, John
Flinn, John
Foot, James
Foot, W[illia]m
Ford, . . .
Ford, Abr[aha]m
Fort, Tho[ma]s
Foudery, Sam[uel]
Fox, W[illia]m
Freize, Henry
Freyar, W[illia]m
Frisby, Sarah, Estate
Fudrey, John
Fullim, William
Fussell, Jacob
Fussell, Solomon

Galbreath, Rob[er]t
Galbreadth, Rob[er]t, Jr.
Galbreath, Sam[uel]
Gallaway, W[illia]m
Gardner, Zach[a]r[ia]h
Garrand, Tho[ma]s
Garrett, John, Esq.
Garrett, John, Jr.
Garrett, William
Garretson, Peter
Garritson, Elik[a]m
Garritson, Henry
Garritson, James
Geddes, Henry
Geddes, W[illia]m
Gibbons, James, Esq.
Gibson, Edw[ar]d
Gibson, Tho[ma]s, Estate

Giffin, John
Giffin, Rob[er]t
Giffins, Tho[ma]s, Estate
Gilliland, James
Gilliss, Marg[are]t, Estate
Gilmer, James
Gilmer, Rob[er]t
Gilpin, . . . , Estate
Gilpin, Ann, Estate
Gilpin, Edw[ard]
Gilpin, Jos[eph]
Gilpin, Joseph, Jr.
Gilpin, Tho[ma]s, Estate
Gilpin, Vinc[en]t
Given, . . . , cordwainer
Given, James
Given, W[illia]m
Goldan, Phillip
Golde, Strange
Gossett, John
Grantham, Charles
Graves, David
Graves, Jacob
Graves, Sam[ue]l
Gray, John
Green, Rob[er]t, Estate
Gregg, Abr[aha]m
Gregg, Harmon, Estate
Gregg, Isaac, and Estate
Gregg, John
Gregg, Joseph, Estate
Gregg, Sam[uel]
Gregg, Silas
Gregg, Tho[ma]s
Gregg, William
Grimes, Richard
Grubb, John
Gunn, Henry
Gunn, Tho[ma]s

Hains, Corn[elius]
Hall, Joseph
Hallowell, Josh[u]a
Hamilton, Charles
Hamilton, James
Hamilton, Rob[er]t.
Hamilton, Tho[ma]s
Hanson, Eliz[abet]h, Estate
Hanson, Timot[h]y
Hardin, Peter
Harp, John
Harriss, Barny C.
Harriss, Jesse
Harriss, Joseph
Hartley, Benj[amin], Estate

Hartt, John
Harvey, James
Harvey, Job
Harvey, Mary, Estate
Harvy, Jonat[ha]n
Hawke, And[re]w
Hayes, John
Hayes, Step[he]n, Jr.
Hayes, Step[he]n, Sr.
Hazley, . . .
Heald, Jacob
Heald, Sam[ue]l
Hedges, Joseph
Hemphill, William
Hendericson, David
Henderson, Thomas
Hendrickson, David
Hendrickson, Isaac
Hendrickson, John
Hendrickson, John, Jr.
Hendrickson, Peter
Hendrickson, Peter, Jr.
Hendrickson, Zach[a]r[ia]h
Hershey, Henry
Hewes, Edw[ard]
Hill, James
Hill, John
Hinshen, Charles
Hodges, And[re]w, Estate
Hogg, And[re]w
Hogg, Sam[ue]l, Jr.
Hogg, Sam[ue]l, Sr.
Hollingsworth, Amor
Hollingsworth, Christ[ophe]r
Hollingsworth, Isaac
Hollingsworth, Jehu
Hollingsworth, Jehu, Jr.
Hollingsworth, John
Hollingsworth, Levi
Hollingsworth, Sam[ue]l
Hollingsworth, Tho[ma]s
Hollingsworth, Tho[ma]s, Jr.
Hood, James, Estate
Hood, John
Horn, John
Horner, Sam[ue]l
Howell, George
Howran, Edw[ard]
Hughes, Isaac
Hughs, David, Estate
Hughs, Rob[er]t
Hunter, Charles
Hunter, Tho[ma]s
Husbands, James
Hutchison, Rob[er]t

Hutchison, W[illia]m
Hyland, Henry, Estate

Isherwood, Able
Israel, Lawrans

Jackson, Eliz[abet]h, Gabe's wife
Jackson, Isaac
Jackson, James
Jackson, Josh[u]a
Jackson, Timot[h]y
Jaquett, Peter, Sr., Estate
Jefferis, James
Jefferis, John
Jennett, Matth[ew]
Jefferis, Tho[ma]s
Jennett, Christ[ophe]r
Johns, Heth, Estate
Johnson, Daniel
Johnson, Henry
Johnson, Hump[h]ry, Estate
Johnson, John, cur[r]i[e]r
Johnson, Simon, Estate
Johnson, William, Estate
Johnston, Henry
Jones, Amos
Jones, John, Estate
Jones, Phillip, Estate
Jones, Rob[er]t
Jones, Tho[ma]s, cordwainer
Jones, William
Jordan, James
Jordan, James, Jr.
Justis, John, Estate
Justis, Jonas
Justis, Peter, Estate
Justis, Swain, Estate

Kean, James
Kean, Tho[ma]s, Esq., Estate
Keen, John
Kenady, James, Estate
Kendall, John
Kenney, Jacob
Killan, James
Kindall, Isaac
Kindall, James
King, Edw[ard]
Kirk, Calib
Kirk, Calib, Sr.
Kirk, John
Kirk, Jonat[ha]n, Estate
Kirk, Kirk
Kirk, Tho[ma]s
Kirk, W[illia]m

Kirkpatrick, George
Kirkpatrick, John
Kirkpatrick, Sam[ue]l
Knott, Joseph

Laing, Benj[amin]
Lake, John
Langley, John
Langley, Tho[ma]s
Latimer, Henry, Esq.
Latimer, James, Esq.
Latimer, Thomas
Lawrence, Isaac
Lawson, Joseph
Lea, James, Jr.
Lea, James, Sr.·
Lea, John, Esq.
Leaforge, Benjamin
Lewdin, John, Estate
Lewis, Curtis
Lewis, Sam[ue]l, Estate
Lightbody, Michael
Lightfoot, Tho[ma]s
Lightfoot, William, Estate
Lissley, Curtis
Little, Archib[a]ld
Little, Robert
Little, Tho[ma]s, Estate
Littler, Tho[ma]s
Lobb, Joseph
Lobb, Joshua
Lownes, Hugh, Estate
Lownes, Mary, Estate
Lownes, Sarah, Estate
Lowrey, Rob[er]t
Lynam, John
Lynam, Phillip
Lyttle, Sam[ue]l

McBrides, Sam[ue]l, Estate
McCalley, James
McCalley, Robert
McCalmont, David
McCalmont, John, Estate
McCleland, James, Estate
McCleland, James, Sr., Estate
McCleland, Joseph, Estate
McClogg, Sam[ue]l
McCloosky, . . . , coop[e]r
McCloud, . . . , Estate
McCloud, John
McCloud, Richard
McCollum, James
McComb, Elizr. [Eleazer], Esq.
McConahan, Fran[ci]s

McConahey, John
McConnall, John
McCord, Richard, Estate
McCorkell, James
McCowan, Edw[ard]
McCracken, Alex[ande]r
McCrackin, John
McCullough, James, and Estate
McDonnall, John
McDowell, Sarah, Estate
McElwain, John
McGarrah, Rob[er]t
McGinnis, Casparus, Estate
McGlashan, John
McGonagle, Phillip
McKee, William
McKever, Hugh
McKinly, John, Esq.
McKnight, James
McKnight, John
McKnight, Rob[er]t
McKnly, Fran[ci]s
McLane, Benj[amin]
McLane, Charl[es]
McNeal, Valentine

Man, Sam[ue]l, Estate
Mans, Hugh, Jr.
Margary, Hugh
Marrott, Joseph
Marrott, Tho[ma]s
Marshall, James, Estate
Marshall, John
Marshall, William, Estate
Martin, John
Mason, . . . , Capt., Estate
Mason, John, Estate
Mason, Richard, Estate
Mason, Thomas, Estate
Matheis, William
Matson, Jonas
Matson, Moses
Matthews, George
Maulin, Richard
May, Tho[ma]s, Esq.
May, W[illia]m
Means, Hugh
Mendinghall, Benjamin
Mendinghall, Tho[ma]s
Mendinhall, Eli
Mendinhall, Isaac
Meredith, Joseph
Meredith, Tho[ma]s, Estate
Meredith, Walter

Merriss, Joseph, Estate
Mettz, Henry
Miers, Jacob
Milener, John
Miliner, Nathan
Miliner, Sam[uel]
Millar, David
Millar, Rob[er]t
Millar, Thomas
Miller, John
Milleland, David
Minshall, Ann, Estate
Minshall, Griffith
Montgomery, Hugh, Capt.
Montgomery, James
Moore, Henry
Moore, James
Moore, John
Moore, Richard, Estate
Moore, Samuel P.
Moore, William
Moorehead, Sam[ue]l, Estate
Morland, Richard
Morriss, Andrew
Morriss, Job
Morrow, Mikl. [Michael]
Morton, [Joseph]
Morton, Robert, Estate
Morton, Sam[ue]l, Estate
Mullan, James
Murdock, Patrick, Estate
Murray, Dan[ie]l, Estate

Naff, Hance, Jr.
Naff, Hance, Sr.
Naff, Henry
Nebucar, John
Neill, John
Neill, William
Newlin, Cyrus
Newlin, Ellis
Newlin, Nath[anie]l
Nibucar, Henry
Nichols, Tmor
Nichols, Sam[ue]l
Nichols, Tho[ma]s, & Son
Niles, Hez[e]k[iah]h
Nilson, David
Nilson, George, Estate
Norred, Dan[ie]l
Nox, Gilbert

Obford, John
O'Flinn, Patrick

Ogle, Charl[es]
Ogle, Thomas, Estate
Osburn, James
Osburn, Peter, Estate
Osburn, Sam[ue]l, Estate
Oston, Tho[ma]s, cooper
Otley, Abner

Painter, Sam[ue]l
Park, John
Parke, David
Parker, James
Parks,   . . . , Capt.
Paschall, Henry
Patterson, Thomas
Paulson, Charl[es]
Paulson, Jacob
Paulson, John, Estate
Paulson, Levi
Paulson, Peter
Payne, John
Peach, Tho[ma]s
Peach, William
Pearce, Jehu
Pearce, Jesse
Pearce, John
Pearson, Joseph
Peirce, Jesse
Peirce, Robert, Jr.
Peirce, Robert, Sr.
Peirsson, Isack
Pennock, Lewis, Estate
Petterman, Benj[amin]
Petterman, George
Petterson, John
Phillips, John, Estate
Phillips, John, millright
Phillips, Nath[anie]l
Phillips, Robert
Phillips, Sam[ue]l
Phillips, William, Estate
Pluright, John
Pluright, William
Poole, Joseph, Estate
Poole, William
Porter, Alxr. [Alexander]
Preston, Jonas
Preston, William
Pritchard, Jesse
Pyle, Jonath[a]n
Pyle, Joseph

Quain, Thomas
Quintence, Joseph

Rambo, And[re]w
Rambo, Daniel
Rambo, John
Rambo, Randall
Rankin, John
Ray, John, Estate
Ray, Moses
Redmond, John
Reynolds, Abr[aha]m
Reynolds, Henry
Reynolds, Joseph
Reynolds, Tho[ma]s
Rice, Henry
Rice, Tho[ma]s
Rice, William
Richards, Jesse
Richards, Nath[anie]l
Richards, Tho[ma]s
Richardson, John
Richardson, Mary, Estate
Richardson, Nicholas
Richardson, Richard
Richardson, Sarah, Estate
Richmond, Sam[ue]l
Roberts, Griffith
Robinett, John
Robinson, Fran[ci]s
Robinson, Israel
Robinson, Job
Robinson, Jacob
Robinson, James, Estate
Robinson, James, Jr.
Robinson, John
Robinson, Jonat[ha]n, Estate
Robinson, Nichols
Robinson, Robert, Estate
Robinson, Rob[er]t, weaver
Robinson, Tho[ma]s
Robinson, William
Rodgers, John
Romsey, Tho[ma]s
Rothwell, Benj[amin], Estate
Rumford, Jonath[a]n
Russell, James
Russell, Robert
Ruth, Adam

Sainsfield, John
Scothorn, Isaac
Scothorn, John
Scott, Absol[a]m
Seal, Caleb
Seal, Josh[u]a
Sellars, George

Sellars, Jacob
Sellars, John
Sellars, Nichols
Servis, John
Sevager, Morris
Sewell, Stephen, Estate
Shackman, George
Shallcross, John
Shallcross, Joseph, Jr.
Shallcross, Joseph, Sr.
Shallcross, Thomas
Sharp, Sam[uel]
Sharp, William
Sharpless, Caleb
Sharpless, Tho[ma]s, Estate
Sharpley, Isaac
Sheward, Benj[amin]
Sheward, Caleb, Estate
Sheward, James
Shipley, John
Shipley, Joseph
Shipley, Sam[ue]l
Shiply, Tho[ma]s, Estate
Shipley, William
Simmonds, John
Simmonds, William
Simoson, William
Simpson, Robert
Sinnex, Henry
Sinnex, Thomas
Sinnix, And[re]w
Sinnix, Tho[ma]s
Sinnix, Tho[ma]s
Slaymaker, Math[ia]s
Sliver, Phillip
Sloan, James
Smith, Ann, Estate
Smith, Ebenezer
Smith, Fran[ci]s, Estate
Smith, George
Smith, James
Smith, Richard
Smith, Tho[ma]s
Smith, William, and Estate
Sorrell, John, Estate
Spencer, John
Sperry, John
Spilman, Phillip
Springer, Charl[es]
Springer, Gabr[ie]l, Estate
Springer, Jacob, Estate
Springer, James
Springer, Jehu
Springer, John

Springer, John, Jr.
Springer, Joseph
Springer, Joseph, Jr.
Springer, Levi
Springer, Peter
Springer, Slator
Springer, William
Stallcop, Peter, Estate
Stamcast, Hance
Stapler, John
Starr, Isaac
Starr, Isaac, Jr.
Starr, William, Estate
Starr, William, Jr.
Starrett, Rob[er]t
Stedham, Cornel[iu]s
Stedham, Henry
Stedham, John, Jr.
Stedham, Jonas, bricklayer
Stedham, Jonas, Jr.
Stedham, Jonas, Sr.
Stedham, Joseph
Stern, George
Stidham, John
Stidham, John, Jr.
Stilly, And[re]w
Stilly, John
Stilly, John, Jr.
Stinson, James
Stone, Lewis
Stoops, George
Stroud, Able
Stroud, Tho[ma]s
Stunkard, James
Sumerell, Joseph

Tally, Jacob
Tanyard, John
Tate, Levi
Tate, William
Tatnall, Joseph, Estate
Taylor, George
Taylor, John
Taylor, Rob[er]t
Taylor, William
Temple, William
Thomas, Arthur
Thomas, Hugh
Thomas, Jesse
Thomas, Joseph
Thomson, Hugh
Thomson, John
Thomson, Nath[anie]l
Thomson, Sam[uel]
Thomson, William, weaver

Tilton, Nemih. [Nehemiah]
Todd, Josh[u]a
Todd, Tho[ma]s
Tomlinson, John, Estate
Tomlinson, Joseph
Townsend, Joseph
Toy, John
Tripp, John
Troth, Henry
Tryon, David, Estate
Tussey, William, Estate

Underwood, Isaac
Underwood, Jos[eph]
Underwood, Sam[uel]
Underwood, William

Vaneman, Andrew
Vaneman, John, Jr., and Estate
Vaneman, William, Estate
Vanport, James
Vertt, Fred[eric]k
Vickrey, . . .
Vining, John, b. s.
Virance, Fred[eric]k

Walfe, Mikl. [Michael], Jr.
Walker, And[re]w, Estate
Walker, Ralph
Wallace, John
Wallace, Sam[uel]
Wallace, Thomas, and Estate
Walraven, Jesse
Walraven, Justa
Walraven, Levi
Walraven, Lucas
Walraven, Peter
Walraven, Walraven
Walsh, John
Walsh, Marg[are]t, Estate
Walters, John
Walter, William
Walters, William, Jr.
Warner, Joseph
Watson, Tho[ma]s
Watt, John
Wattles, And[re]w
Way, Caleb
Way, Fran[ci]s
Way, John, and Estate
Way, Joseph, Jr., Estate
Way, Joseph, Sr., Estate
Way, Nichols
Weaver, Henry
Webster, John

Weldon, James
Welsh, John
West, Joseph
Whaler, James
White, John
White, Peter
White, William
Whitelock, Charl[es], Estate
Whitelock, Isaac, Estate
Whitzell, George
Wilkinson, Dan[iel]
Wilkinson, Joseph, Estate
Wilkinson, Thomas
Wilkinson, William
Williams, John
Williams, Tho[ma]s, Estate
Williams, Tho[ma]s
Williamson, Adam
Williamson, George
Willis, William
Wilson, Carson
Wilson, Christ[ophe]r, Estate
Wilson, Ezek[ie]l
Wilson, George
Wilson, Isaac
Wilson, Stephen
Wilson, Tho[ma]s, and Estate
Wilson, Tho[ma]s, Jr.
Wilson, William, and Estate
Windle, David, Estate
Wingate, Dan[ie]l
Wood, John
Wood, Nathan
Wood, William
Woodburn, James
Woodcock, Bancroft
Woodcock, Isaac
Woodcock, Rebec[c?a, Estate
Woodcock, Sam[ue]l
Woodcock, William
Woodward, Mordic]i[a
Wooliston, Joshua
Woolston, Benj[amin]
Woolston, Jerem[ia]h
Worell, John
Wormsley, Thomas, Estate
Wright, Fran[ci]s

Yarnall, Benj[amin]
Yarnall, Eliz[abet]h, Estate
Yarnall, Est[he]r, Estate
Yarnall, John
Yearnest, And[re]w
Yeatman, Andrew
Yeatman, John

Yeats, John

Young, Nath[anie]l

Zane, Joel

Zane, Jon[a]t[ha]n

MILL CREEK HUNDRED

Adams, John

Alexander, John

Alexander, William

Alison, James

Ayger, James

Ayger, Robert

Bacon, John

Ball, James

Ball, John

Ball, Joseph

Ball, Martha, Estate

Barker, Samuel

Barr, John

Barton, John

Barton, Sarah

Barton, William

Bartram, Moses, Estate

Bason, John

Bell, James, Estate

Best, Valentine

Bishop, Elizabeth

Bishop, John

Bishop, Nicholas

Black, James, Esq.

Black, John

Boggs, James

Boggs, Moses

Boggs, Robert

Boice, John

Boyce, Robert, Estate

Braken, Henry

Brakon, William

Brokin, John

Brown, Alexander

Bruce, John

Burk, John

Burk, John, Jr.

Burns, Caleb

Burns, James

Burns, Joseph

Caldwell, Nivans, Estate

Canby, Thomas

Cannon, Joseph

Carlisle, Samuel

Castalo, William

Chambers, Joseph

Chandler, George

Chandler, Isaac

Chandler, Spencer

Chesnot, John

Clark, James

Clements, Forgus

Cloud, William

Cochran, Stephen, Estate

Cochran, Thomas

Cooper, Hugh

Corry, William

Craford, Robert

Craghead, George, Esq.

Credick, William

Creighton, Robert

Cross, David

Crossan, James

Crossan, Samuel

Crossan, William

Daniel, Alexander

Daniel, John

Dickinson, John, Esq., Estate

Dixson, Enoch, Estate

Dixson, James

Dixson, Jehu

Dixson, John, Estate

Dixson, Philips, Estate

Dixson, Thomas

Douglass, David

Drummon, Joseph

Dunkan, Patrick

Eddy, William

Eliot, John

Ely, Michael

England, Joseph

English, Sarah

Evans, Charles, Estate

Evans, Evan, Estate

Evans, John

Evans, Oliver

Evans, William

Faran, William

Fergison, Hugh

Ferguson, Thomas

Fitzsimmons, John

Foot, John

Foot, William

Ford, Alexander

Ford, David

Ford, Frederick

Garnor, John

Garrat, John, Esq., Estate

Giffon, Mathew

Giffon, Robert

Gillahan, William

Gilmore, John
Graham, John, smith
Graham, John, weaver
Graham, William
Graves, Johnathan, Estate
Graves, Samuel, Estate
Gray, Marg[a]ret
Green, Thomas
Gregg, Hermon, Estate
Gregg, John
Gregg, Silas
Gregg, William
Grub[b], George
Grub[b], Richard
Guthry, Alexander
Guthry, Alexander, Jr.
Guthry, William
Hadly, John
Hadly, Simon
Hamilton, George
Hamilton, John
Hannah, James
Hannah, John
Hanway, John
Hanway, Thomas
Hardman, John
Harland, William
Harlin, Caleb
Hassan, William
Hayes, Eliot
Heald, Samuel
Henderson, Joseph
Henderson, Robert
Henry, David
Hersey, Solomon
Hewes, David, Estate
Hewes, Isack
Hewes, Robert
Hiland, Henry, Estate
Holmes, Abraham
Hoops, David, Estate
Hoops, Thomas
Hulot, Joseph
Huston, Samuel
Jackson, James
James, John
James, John, Esq., Estate
John, Enoch, Estate
John, Heath
John, Malichia
John, William
Johnston, Robert
Johnston, William, carpenter
Johnston, William (Milltown)
Jordan, James
Jordan, John, and Estate

Jordan, Samuel
Jordan, William
Justis, Andrew
Justis, Jacob
Justis, Swain
Kelly, Samuel
Kenny, Moses
Kerns, Richard
Langley, Thomas
Lattimer, George, Esq., Estate
Lea, Thomas
Lewis, David, Estate
Lindsey, John
Lindsey, Samuel
Lindsey, William
Lisle, James
Lockard, John
Lord, James
McAntire, Samuel
McBeath, John
McClenahan, Eligah
McCormack, David
McCulluch, George
McDonald, Archibald, Jr.
McDonald, Archibald, Sr.
McDonald, Hannah
McDonald, James
McDonald, Thomas
McDouch, Arthur
McElwaine, Andrew
McElwee, William
McEntire, John
McFerson, Robert
McKennon, James
McKnight, Moses
McKrea, Thomas
McKrory, John
McMullin, Archibald
McWhortor, Hewes, Estate
MacCormac, John
MacCormack, John, Jr.
Magee, John
Magregor, Hewes
Magyre, Thomas
Mahan, Francis
Mahan, Richard
Marshall, James, Estate
Marshall, William
Martin, John, Estate
Matire, Thomas
Mecer, David
Mendingall, Aaron
Mendingall, James
Montgomery, Alexander, Estate
Montgomery, Daniel
Montgomery, David

Montgomery, James, (Samuel's son)
Montgomery, Robert
Montgomery, Samuel
Montgomery, Thomas
Montgomery, Thomas, Esq.
Montgomery, William
Moore, Jacob
Moore, William, Estate
Morgan, William
Morison, Robert, Estate
Mullinix, Robert Priest, Estate
Murren, Henry
Nabicor, John
Nevins, John
Nicholas, Daniel
Nicholas, Ellis
Oagal, James, Estate
Ocheltree, James
Paterson, Andrew
Paterson, John, Jr.
Pearce, Isaach
Pearson, Thomas
Penington, Edward, Estate
Philips, James
Philips, John
Philips, Joseph
Philips, Robert, Estate
Philips, William
Philips, William, Jr.
Pollock, James
Poulston, Andrew, Estate
Poulston, Simon
Pyle, John
Pyles, Samuel
Quillin, Nathan
Reynalds, Alexander
Rice, Evans, Esq., Estate
Rice, Evenas, Esq., Estate
Rice, Ezekiel, Estate
Rice, James, and Estate
Rice, Jeremiah
Rice, John, farmer
Rice, John, miller
Rice, Joseph
Rice, Solomon
Rice, Thomas
Rice, Thomas, Jr., Estate
Richey, James
Robinson, Jacob
Robinson, Jacob, Estate
Robinson, James
Robinson, John
Robinson, Joseph
Robinson, Joseph, farm[er]
Ross, James
Ross, John, Estate

Sample, William
Sanders, Amos
Servis, John
Shad, Hance
Sharples, Caleb, Estate
Sharples, Jacob
Sharples, Joseph
Sheakspear, Samuel
Short, James
Simonton, John, Estate
Simonton, William
Smith, Henry
Smith, Samuel, Estate
Smith, William
Springer, Benjamin
Springer, Charles, Jr.
Springer, Christopher
Springer, Jerrmiah
Springer, Nicholas
Springer, Thomas
Star, Jacob
Stepler, Henry
Stepler, John, Estate
Stepler, Thomas
Stepler, William
Stroud, George
Stroud, James
Stroud, Joshua
Stuart, William
Swan, Robert
Tate, ———, widow
Taylor, George
Theophilus, John, Estate
Thomas, Evan
Thomas, Joseph
Thomson, Daniel
Thomson, John
Tool, Arthur
Vincent, Clark John
Walker, David
Walker, John
Walker, Joseph
Wallis, Thomas
Warten, Cha[rle]s Henry, Estate
Watt, John
Way, John, Estate
Way, Thomas
Web, Joseph
Weldon, George
Wells, Harrison
Whitey, John
Wholahan, John
Wilason, James
Williams, Charles
Williams, Jonathan, Estate
Williamson, David

Wilson, James
Wilson, Stephen
Wilson, William, farm [e]r
Wilson, W[illia]m, wheelwright
Wims, John, Colonel, Estate
Winder, James
Winder, John
Withrow, Samuel, Estate
Wolason, George

Wolason, William
Wood, Elizabeth, Estate
Woodard, Henry
Woodcock, Samuel
Woolson, Jacob
Woolson, Thomas
Yernall, Ephiram
Yernall, Jonathan

NEW CASTLE HUNDRED

Aiken, Robert
Aiken, Samuel, Rev., Estate
Aiken, Thomas
Aiken, William
Aiken, William, tailor
Alexander, Archibald
Alrich, Lucas
Alrich, Sigfiedes, Estate
Armstrong, Christopher
Armstrong, Robert
Ashley, Richard
Barr, Robert
Barr, Samuel
Bedford, Gunning, Esq.
Bedford, Gunning, Estate
Bedford, William
Belvell, Jacob
Betson, Stephen
Blackburn, William, Estate
Blankford, John
Boggs, Joseph
Bole, George
Bond, John, Estate
Bool, John
Booth, James, Esq.
Booth, John, Jr.
Booth, Robert
Bouden, James
Bringhurst, James, Estate
Broom, Abraham
Brown, John
Bryan, Robert, and Estate
Burns, John
Caldwell, James
Camel, Neal
Canady, John
Canney, James
Cannon, Abraham
Cannon, Isaac
Carter, James
Caulk, William G.
Champion, James, Estate
Clark, John, Estate
Clay, Thomas

Clay, William
Cloe, Abraham
Cloe, Jacob
Colesberry, Henry
Colesberry, Jacob
Colesberry, Levi
Cooch, Thomas, Estate
Cook, Jacob
Coulter, John
Coulter, William
Craig, John
Creighton, William
Cross, Samuel
Crow, John
Croxall, Charles
Cuningham, John
Darby, Henry
Deckart, James
Delany, Michael
Deniston, Thomas
Derrickson, David
Device, James
Devilon, James
Devoe, Devid
Devoe, Frederick and father's Estate
Devoe, Isaac
Doke, Matthew
Dorrity, David
Doulin, Samuel
Doulin, William
Duncan, Alexander
Dushane, Anthony, Estate
Dushane, Benjamin
Dyatt, Adam
Elliott, William
Enos, John
Evans, John
Eves, James, and Estate
Ewing, John, Estate
Farron, Edward
Femister, Alexander
Finney, David, Esq.
Finney, John, Dr., Estate
Fisher, Samuel

Fopless, John
Frazier, William
Furnis, Robert, Estate
Garretson, Eliakim, Estate
Garretson, James
Gibson, James
Gilbert, Stephen
Gilpin, Vincent, Estate
Goften, Charles
Gorman, David
Grantham, Isaac, Esq.
Gregory, Benjamin
Guyer, Adam, Estate
Hains, Isaac
Haisley, James
Hall, Alexander
Hall, Chambers
Hall, Joel
Hanna, John, Estate
Hanna, Samuel
Harp, David
Harslet, William
Harvey, Alexander
Harvey, Job, Estate
Heggins, Jesse, Estate
Henry, John
Hickman, John
Hill, Frederick
Hinsey, Cornelius
Hinsey, John
Hinsey, John, Jr.
Howel, Benjamin
Hunn, ———, Capt., Estate
Irwin, David
Irwin, David, weaver
Israel, Israel, Estate
Jamison, Alexander
Jamison, William
Janvier, Francis
Janvier, Philip, Sr., Estate
Janvier, Richard, Estate
Janvier, Thomas
Jaquet, Hance, Estate
Jaquet, John
Jaquet, John, Jr.
Jaquet, Nicholas
Jaquet, Peter, and Estate
Jaquet, Thomas, Estate
Johns, Kensey, Esq., and Estate
Jones, Cantwell, Estate
Jones, Thomas
Kean, John
Kemster, George
Kenear, James
Kerns, John, Dr.

Kerr, Robert
King, Andrew
King, George
King, John, Estate
King, Michael
Kirk, Isaac
Kirk, John
Lackey, James
Lackey, John, Estate
Laferty, Francis
Land, John
Land, William, Estate
Lees, William
Levingston, Michael
Lewdon, John, and Estate
Lewdon, John, tanner
Lewis, Joel, Estate
Lewis, Joseph
Lindon, Jeston
Lockart, Joseph
Lollar, Thomas
McCart, John
McClay, Barney
McClay, James
McClay, John, Estate
McClintock, William
McCook, James
McCormick, Patrick
McCreary, Isaac
McCreden, Charles
McCullo, James, weaver
McCullough, James
McDade, Daniel
McGahey, William
McGarvey, William
McGee, Thomas
McGinnes, Patrick
McGloven, Patrick
McGuire, Denis
McGuire, Thomas
McKean, Thomas, Estate
McKinsey, John
McLarney, William
McLonan, Agness, Estate
McMechen, William, Dr., Estate
McPherson, John
McWilliam, Richard, Estate
McWilliams, Rebekah, Estate
Macky, Esther, Estate
Mann, Isaiah
Mann, William
Mann, William, Jr.
Maxwell, ———, Estate
Maxwell, Robert, Estate
Maxwell, Solomon, Estate

Mears, Robert, Estate
Meridith, Reece, Estate
Midleton, Robert, Estate
Millegan, William
Miller, Andrew, Estate
Miller, John
Milligan, Hugh
Milligan, James
Minor, Thomas
Monro, George, Estate
Montgomery, Alexander
Montgomery, Alex[and]r, Esq., Estate
Montooth, Henry
Moony, Thomas
Moore, Thomas
Morrison, John
Morrison, William
Morton, Andrew
Morton, Ebenezer, Estate
Morton, Mathias
Morton, Morton
Mullan, Hugh
Mullen, Edward
Musgrove, Job
Nesbett, Thomas
Pasmore, John, Estate
Patridge, James
Patten, Alexander
Patton, David
Peirce, George
Peirce, Matthew, Esq.
Peirce, Robert, Estate
Penton, Renier
Perry, Joshua
Peterson, Jacob
Pike, Stephen
Polk, Stephen
Poole, Samuel
Porter, Alexander, Esq., and Estate
Porter, Charles, Estate
Porter, David, Estate
Price, John
Read, George, Esq.
Read, George, Jr.
Reed, Alexander
Reynolds, George, and Estate
Reynolds, John
Rezoe, Benjamin
Rezoe, James, Estate
Rezou, James
Rhoads, Joseph
Rhoads, Richard
Rhoads, Thomas
Riddle, James
Rotherham, Jacob

Rowan, Samuel
Ruth, John
Ruth, Samuel
Ruth, William
Sample, William, Estate
Sankey, Abraham, Estate
Sankey, George, Estate
Scott, William
Shafley, Joseph
Shields, Robert, and Estate
Shields, Thomas, Estate
Short, Abraham
Silsbee, John
Simenton, John, Estate
Slator, ———, widow, Estate
Smith, Andrew
Smith, Gasper
Smith, Thomas
Spotswood, William
Stalcop, Peter, Estate
Sterrett, Alexander
Steuart, John, Estate
Stidham, Isaac
Stidham, Lucas
Stidham, Peter
Stidham, William
Stoekton, John, Esq.
Stockton, John, Estate
Stoop, Ephraim
Sullinger, William
Sutton, Thomas
Tatlow, Joseph, Esq.
Thompson, David, Dr., Estate
Thompson, Robert
Thompson, Steuart
Toland, James
Toland, John
Toland, William
Turner, Daniel, Estate
Turner, Nathan
Turner, Thomas
Twedy, David
Van Gezel, John
Van Leiuvangh, Catherine, Estate
Van Leveneigh, Zachariah, Estate
VanSant, Asa
Walls, Nicholas, Estate
Watson, James
Watts, John
Webb, Jacob
Welsh, Morton
Wethered, John
Wharten, Charles, Estate
White, Thomas

Wiley, Robert, Estate
Williams, Morris, Estate
Wirt, George

Yard, Isaiah
Yeates, Donaldson, Estate
Yeates, John

PENCADER HUNDRED

Adair, Richard
Adams, George
Aikin, Mathew
Akin, James
Alexander, Elinor, Estate
Allin, Samuel
Armstrong, Archabald
Armstrong, Robert
Balews, Jacob, Estate
Bartholomew, Thomas
Barvard, Benjamin, Estate
Biddle, John
Bird, George
Black, William, Estate
Boldin, Elisha
Boldin, James
Boldin, James, Jr.
Boldin, Levy
Boldin, Nathan
Boldin, Thomas
Boldin, Thomas, Jr.
Booth, Jonathan, Estate
Bowin, John
Bradly, Thomas
Bradly, William
Brady, James
Brady, Samuel
Brooks, John
Brown, George
Bunker, William
Camblin, John
Camblin, William
Carpentor, Vallentine
Cavender, Alexander
Clark, Henry
Clark, John, cordwainer
Clark, William, Estate
Clinton, Thomas
Conn, Joseph
Cooch, Thomas, Esq., Estate
Cooch, William
Cozier, Jacob
Craferd, John
Cummins, William
David, Evin, carpenter
David, Joseph, Estate
David, Joshua
David, Thomas
Davis, Abel, Estate
Davis, Benjamin

Davis, David, Estate
Davis, Judiah
Divinney, Felix
Duallins, David, Estate
Dunlap, James
Dushane, Anthony, Estate
Elder, John
Evans, Evan
Evans, George
Evans, Isaac
Evans, Joel
Evans, John, Jr.
Evans, John, and Estate
Evans, Nathan[i]el
Evans, Peter, Estate
Evans, Thom[a]s, Dr.
Faris, Isiah
Faris, Jacob
Faris, James
Faris, John
Faris, Jonah W[illia]m
Faris, Samu[e]l
Faris, William, Estate
Fisher, Andrew
Flood, Joseph
Fryer, Samuel
Gallaher, James
Gallaher, William
Gean, Samuel, Esq., Estate
Gess, Cristopher
Glann, Thomas
Griffith, James
Griffith, Richard
Grifith, Griffy
Grifith, John
Gutry, Robert
Guttry, Samuel
Haise, Benjamin
Haise, David
Hall, George
Hall, William
Hambleton, William
Handlin, Alexander
Hanon, George
Hanon, Thomas
Harvey, Job, Estate
Henderson, John
Henderson, Thomas
Hinchman, Adam
Hollon, John, cooper

Hollond, Isaac
Houghey, Robert, Estate
Houhey, William
Howel, David
Huchison, Samuel, Estate
Hukill, Jesse
Hukill, Spencer
Jack, John
Jac[k]son, Jacob
James, James, Estate
James, John
James, Thomas, Estate
Jameson, John
Jankin, Thomas
John, Jehu
John, Joseph
Johnston, James
Johnston, Levi
Jones, Daniel
Jones, Enoch, Estate
Jones, John, and Estate
Jones, Morgan
Keetly, Francis
Kelly, Thomas
King, William
Kinkead, James
Koarrs, Andrew, Estate
Lewis, Richard, Estate
McAntire, Samuel
McAntire, Robert, Estate
McCray, William, Dr.
McKinley, George
McLain, Archibald
McMahans, David, Estate
McMulin, Benjamin
McMullin, James
McMullin, Robert
McMurfys, Robert, Estate
Macolistor, Cristophir
Macord, John
Magin, John
Makinly, Samuel
Mann, John
Middleton, Robert
Miller, Hance
Minor, Moses, Estate
Mitchel[l], Henry
Moore, Alexander
Moore, Jesse
Moore, John
Moore, Robert
Moore, William
Morgin, James
Morrow, Thomas
Morton, Ebinizer

Muldrock, David
Muldrock, John, Estate
O'Hair, Patrick
Paterson, William
Patton, James
Patton, John
Pearce, Henry Ward, Estate
Penngton, Nimrod
Porter, John
Price, James
Price, William
Price, William, Sr.
Prichard, John, Estate
Prichet, Jacob
Raper, James
Redax, William
Reed, John
Rees, David, Estate
Robinson, William
Ross, Aaron, Estate
Runnals, George
Rush, Patrick
Rutherford, John
Shannon, Jerimiah
Shields, Robert, Estate
Smith, Hugh
Smith, Samuel
Smith, Thomas
Stanton, Benjamin
Stanton, John
Stewart, Charles
Stewart, James, Estate
Stoates, John
Taylor, John
Thomas, Acquila, Estate
Thomas, David, Estate
Thomas, John, Dr., Estate
Thomas, Joseph, and Estate
Thomas, Richard
Thomas, William, Estate
Thompson, Alexander
Thompson, Ephram, Estate
Thompson, Mathew
Thompson, Richard, Estate
Thompson, Richard, Jr., Estate
Thompson, Sarah, Estate
Thorson, Richard, Sr., Estate
Twedies, David, Estate
Underwood, John
Underwood, Joseph
Underwood, Nathen
Underwood, Samuel
Underwood, Solomon
Veal, Alexa[n]der
Veasay, Noble

Wagonor, Joseph
Walker, Alexa[n]der
Walker, Andrew
Warnock, David
Warnor, John
Watson, Andrew
Watson, James
Watson, Robert
Watson, Thomas
Weer, Thomas

Weirs, William, Estate
Whan, William
Williams, John
Williams, Nathaniel
Williams, Peter
Williams, Roger
Williams, Thomas
Willson, Hugh
Wirts, Martin, Estate
Yeocem, Charles

RED LION HUNDRED

Adams, Leonard
Adams, Thomas, and Estate
Adams, Tho[ma]s, Jr.
Allen, Robert
Allen, Samuel
Armstrong, James
Armstrong, James, Jr.
Belleby, John, Estate
Boulden, James
Bradley, John
Caldwell, Charles
Caldwell, David
Cannon, Isaac
Carr, Nathaniel
Carrigan, John
Carson, William, Estate
Carson, William, Estate
Cart[e]y, Charles
Clark, John
Clark, Johnathan
Clifford, John
Craven, Thomas
Dick, James
Dick, Robert
Dick, Thomas
Dodd, John
Donnoly, John
Dushane, Abraham
Dushane, Anthony
Dushane, Isaac, Estate
Eccles, Samuel
Floree, Francis
Fullam, Walter
Garritson, John
Gibbons, John
Graven, Peter
Hanson, Nathaniel
Harmon, Hance
Hickey, William
Higgins, Anthony
Higgins, David
Higgins, Jesse

Higgins, Laurence, Estate
Hinton, Thomas
Hinton, William
Howell, Enos, Estate
Hyatt, John, Esq., and Estate
Inglish, Samuel
Jones, Whitehead
Jones, Whitehead and Company
Kelly, William
Kelly, William, weaver
Kettle, Cornelius, Estate
Laurance, Andrew
Long, Samuel
McCool, George
McCormick,
McGonnigal, John
McWhorter, John
Maree, Andrew
Miles, Abel
Miller, Andrew
Miller, at Damascus
Monro, Geo[rge], Dr. and father, Estate
Morgan, John
Morgan, John, Jr.
Morrison, Alexander
Morrison, Hugh, and Estate
Murphy, John
Nuttle, Adams, and Estate
Patrick, John
Pearce, William
Porter, James
Porter, Jonas
Porter, Robert
Prior, John
Rees, Thomas, Estate
Robinson, William
Ross, Mary, Estate
Ryland, John
Scott, William
Shankland, James
Silesbee, Nathaniel, Estate
Smith, Alexander
Smith, Robert

Sutton, John
Sutton, Samuel
Sutton, William
Thomas, David, Dr., and Estate
Thompson, Brice
Thompson, David, Dr., Estate
Thompson, John, Esq., and Estate
Thompson, Thomas

Toppin, John
Toppin, John, Jr.
Toppin, Samuel
VanDegrift, Abraham, Estate
Veazey, Samuel
Wark, Joseph
Wood, John

ST. GEORGES HUNDRED

Acton, Clemant
Addison, Henry, Estate
Aikin, John
Alexander, Joseph
Allrichs, John
Allrichs, Peter, Estate
Allrichs, Wessall
Allston, Abner
Allston, John
Anderson, Alex[ander]
Anderson, Joseph, Estate
Anderson, Mat[t]hew
Anderson, W[illia]m
Andrews, John
Antrem, John
Armstrong, Christopher
Armstrong, Cornelious
Armstrong, George
Aspriel, Joseph
Aull, W[illia]m
Batchelder, David
Beaston, Jacob
Beaston, W[illia]m
Beatell, Thomas
Beattle, Andrew
Beattle, Boulden
Bell, W[illia]m
Belviel, Jacob
Bennett, John
Bennett, W[illia]m, Estate
Bird, W[illia]m, Estate
Blackburn, James
Boardly, Beal, Estate
Booth, Thomas
Boulden, Jacob, Estate
Boushell, Joseph
Boushell, Sluyter, Dr.
Boyce, Boaz
Boyce, Henry
Boyce, W[illia]m
Boyd, Adam
Bradford, Sam[ue]l
Bradford, W[illia]m
Brady, W[illia]m
Bratton, Benj[amin]
Bratton, James

Bratton, Thomas
Brothers, James
Brown, John
Brown, Mathew
Bryan, Andrew, Estate
Bryan, John
Bunker, Benjamin
Bunker, John
Burchard, David
Burchard, David, weaver
Burchard, David, son of Samuel Burchard
Burchard, Isaac
Burchard, Sam[ue]l, Estate
Burgess, John
Burgess, W[illia]m, Estate
Butcher, Benj[amin]
Canary, Thomas
Cann, Robert
Cannon, Jacob, Estate
Carpenter, Rich[ar]d
Carpenter, W[illia]m, Jr.
Carpenter, W[illia]m, Sr.
Carson, W[illia]m, Estate
Chatten, Thomas
Clark, W[illia]m
Clayton, Joshua, Esq.
Clayton, Rich[ar]d, Estate
Cleaves, Nathaniel
Cleaves, Thomas
Clemant, Samuel, Estate
Clover, Peter
Cochron, John
Cochron, John, Jr.
Colhoon, Hugh
Congelton, John
Conner, James
Coole, Elisha
Coombs, Adam
Corbitt, Israel, Estate
Corbitt, John
Corbitt, W[illia]m, and Estate
Covinton, Joshua
Craven, David
Crouden, George
Crout, Peter

Crow, George, Estate
Crow, Owen
Crow, Samuel
Cruson, John
Cruson, Peter
Curry, Henry, Estate
Curry, W[illia]m, and Estate
Darrah, James, Estate
Darrah, John
David, James
Deans, Abraham
Delany, Loyd, Estate
Delany, Mathew
Delany, Sharp, Estate
Derrickson, Jadiah
Derrickson, Luke
Dickenson, John, Estate
Ditchar, Jeremia A.
Dowell, James
Downs, John
Duglass, Archabald
Durraham, Pierce
Dushane, Isaac, Estate
Dushane, Jesse, Estate
Egbirtson, Jacob
Egbirtson, John, Estate
Eliason, Abraham
Eliason, Andrew
Elliss, W[illia]m
Enos, Stephen
Enzor, Joseph, Estate
Evans, Gillshot
Evans, William
Evertson, Evert
Evertson, Jacob
Farmer, Thomas
Ferrall, James
Fleming, Alexander
Floyd, Edmond
Floyd, John
Forster, Henry, Esq., Estate
Fowler, Archabald, Estate
Fowler, Jacob
Fowler, John
Fowlow, Edmond
Frain, Richard
Frayzer, W[illia]m, Estate
Fullam, Thomas
Gallaspy, Nathaniel
Garrison, Edmond
Garrison, Richard
Gauner, Rudolph, Estate
Geers, Ephraim
Giffin, Michael
Gillbreath, Hugh

Glacken, John
Golden, John
Gooding, Abraham
Gooding, Isaac
Gooding, Jacob
Gooding, John
Gooding, Sasanah
Gray, John
Green, Banj[amin]
Griffith, Richard, Estate
Hackett, Daniel
Haggerthy, James
Hair, James
Hair, John
Hair, Joseph
Hair, Mathew
Hall, Clement
Hall, John
Hall, William
Hanes, Daniel
Hanson, James
Hanson, John
Hanson, John, Jr.
Hanson, Peter
Hanson, William
Harlen, Phenias
Harmon, Jacob
Hartt, Joseph, Estate
Hattery, Thomas
Haughey, James, and Estate
Haughey, Levi
Haughey, Robert
Hook, John, Estate
Houston, Jacob
Huchason, Joseph
Hudson, John
Hudson, W[illia]m
Hulans, Samuel
Hunter, Jonathan, Estate
Hurley, John
Hyatt, Abraham
Hyatt, Francis
Hyatt, Isaac
Hyatt, John, Estate
Hyatt, John, Esq., Estate
Hyatt, John Vance
Hyatt, Peter, Esq.
Hyrons, John
Irvin, William
Israel, Joseph
James, James, Estate
James, John, Estate
James, Nathaniel
James, W[illia]m
Jamison, Thomas
Janvier, John

Janvier, Phillip
Jetton, Peter
Johns, Kensey, Estate
Johnston, John
Johnston, William
Jones, Cantwell, Estate
Jones, Richard
Kean, Roger, Estate
Kelly, Alexander
King, Francis
King, Isaac
King, John & Co.
King, Peter
Kitchen, Henry
Kneesberry, Mary
Lafferty, Archabald
Lambert, William
Law, John
Lawson, Peter, Estate
Lea, Robert
Leach, Mary
Louron, Mary
Lourox, Mary, Estate
Loyd, Phrisby & Co.
Lyons, Patrick, Estate
McCabe, John
McCannon, [McKennon], William, Capt.
McCay, John
McClanagin, Blair, Estate
McCoole, John, Estate
McCormick, Arthur
McCoy, John
McDonough, Patrick
McGahy, William
McGhohlen, John
McGommory, Robert
McGraw, Thomas
McGriffin, Robert
McKean, Latitia, Estate
McKenney, Robert
McKonough, Thomas, Esq.
McMurphy, Alexander
McMurphy, Robert, and Estate
McWhorter, David
McWhorter, Robert
Mariss, Benj[amin], minor, Estate
Martin, David
Mathews, Hugh, Esq., Estate
Mathews, Robert, Estate
Matthews, Thomas, land
Maxwell, Robert
Meldram, Robert
Merriott, Benjamin, Dr., Estate
Mersar, Robert
Millagan, Robert, Esq., Estate
Money, Robert

Money, Thomas
Moody, Isaac, Estate
Moody, John
Moore, Francis
Moore, James, and Estate
Moore, Robert
Morrison, Daniel
Morrison, Hugh, Estate
Morton, Archabald
Mountain, ———
Murch, Mathew
Murphy, William
Murrin, Tho[ma]s, Capt.
Naudine, Henry
Newell, W[illia]m
Newgan, Thomas
Newlon, Isaac
Nicerson, John
Nickalson, David
Nickson, Nicholas
Night, John L., Estate
Noxon, Benjamin, Estate
Nuttel, Adam, Estate
Ozburn, Robert, Estate
Ozier, Jacob
Parker, George
Parker, Jonas
Patterson, Thomas
Pearce, George, land
Peery, James
Peery, John
Pennington, Henry
Pennington, James
Pennington, John, Jr.
Pennington, John A.
Penton, Reynar, Estate
Perisett, Nicholas
Peterson, Henry, Dr.
Peterson, Peter
Peugh, Jacob
Piper, James, Estate
Pollard, William, Estate
Powel, Jerrymia
Preston, Jonas, Estate
Price, Edward
Price, Spencer
Price, Thomas
Price, W[illia]m
Read, George
Read, James
Read, Thomas, Rev.
Reading, Phillip, and Estate
Reynolds, Jerymiah
Reynolds, John
Reynolds, Thomas, hatter
Reynolds, Thomas, Jr.

Rice, Thomas
Rice, W[illia]m
Richardson, Joshua, Estate
Roberts, John
Robison, Thomas, Esq., Estate
Rothwell, Ebenezor
Rumsay, William, Estate
Sawyer, John
Sawyer, Joseph
Sawyer, Thomas, Estate
Scott, Perry
Scott, Robert
Seabo, David
See, Abraham, Estate
See, Peter, Jr.
See, William
Shepard, Richard
Siglar, Andrew
Skeer, Jacob
Skeer, John, land
Smith, Sam[uel]
Smith, W[illia]m, Jr.
Starr, Jacob
Starr, John, Jr.
Starr, John, Sr.
Starr, Thomas, Estate
Stauts, Isaac
Stedham, Sarah, Mrs., Estate
Stephens, Isaac
Stewart, Alexander, Estate
Stewart, Alexander, Dr.
Stewart, David, Dr.
Stewart, James
Stewart, Samuel
Stoghton, John, Estate
Stoghton, Martha
Streets, Jacob
Summers, Andrew
Ttate, John, tailor
Tate, John, sawyer
Tennary, Eleazar
Tharp, David
Thomas, David, blacksmith
Thomas, David, Estate
Thomas, Enock
Thomas, Isaac, Estate
Thomas, James
Thomas, Margarett

Thomas, Nathan, Dr.
Thomas, W[illia]m, tailor and Estate
Thompson, John, Esq., Estate
Tobin, John
Tobin, Thomas
Toland, John
Toland, Mary, Estate
V[a]nBebbar, Henry, Estate
V[a]n Degrift, Christopher
V[a] Degrift, Isaac
V[a]n Degrift, Jacob
V[a]n Degrift, Leonard
V[a]n Degrift, Lewis
V[a]n Degrift, Thomas
V[a]n Dyke, Abraham, Estate
V[a]n Dyke, David
V[a]n Dyke, Isaac, Estate
V[a]n Dyke, John
V[a]n Hekal, John
V[a]n Horn, Abraham
V[a]n Horn, Jacob
V[a]n Leudnar, Jacob
Vance, Adam
Vance, John, minor, land
Vance, Joseph
Vann, Peter
Vanzandt, James, Estate
Veach, Ebanezar
Veazy, William
Viel, John
Viel, Thomas
Vohan, John, Estate
Walker, William
Weily, John
Weir, William
Wilkins, George
Williams, Deborah, land
Williams, John
Williams, Martha, land
Willson, Benjamin
Willson, David, and Estate
Willson, Hyrons, Estate
Willson, John
Willson, Richard
Wood, William, Estate
Woods, Isaac
Workman, William, Estate

WHITE CLAY CREEK HUNDRED

Adams, Geo[rge]
Adams, Levi
Adams, Thomas
Allen, Andrew, Estate
Allen, Charles

Allen, John, Estate
Allen, Rob[er]t
Anderson, Alex[ande]r
Anderson, James, Jr.
Anderson, James, Sr.

Anderson, Thomas
Armstrong, Edward
Armstrong, William

Barclay, Jno. [John], Estate
Barr, James
Baxter, William
Bayley, John
Bell, Peter
Bennet, Joseph
Black, James
Black, James, Esq., Estate
Black, John
Blair, W[illia]m, L., Estate
Bradford, Sam[ue]l, Estate
Brown, James
Brown, William
Bryson, Stephen
Bunkard, William
Byrnes, Dan[ie]l, Estate
Byrnes, Joshua

Caldwell, James
Cann, James
Cann, Joseph
Cann, William
Carson, Walter
Chamberlin, Joseph
Chambers, Benjamin
Chambers, John
Chapman, Geo[rge]
Chapman, John
Clark, David, Estate
Clark, James
Clement, James
Clements, William
Cline, Nicholas
Cooch, Thomas, Estate
Couper, James
Cox, Barny
Crawford, James

Davis, Abel
Dawson, William
Denniss, Richard, Estate
Devon, Charles
Dixon, William
Douglass, Rob[er]t
Drummond, Arthur
Dunn, James
Durgan, John

Edwards, Morgan
Enos, Joseph

Ferguson, John
Finley, Tho[ma]s
Foreman, John
Foreman, Moses
Foster, ———, Mr., Estate

Gillespie, Geo[rge], Jr.
Gillespie, Geo[rge], Sr.
Gillin, Phillip
Gillispie, Jane, Estate
Glasford, Abel
Glasford, Hugh
Glasgow, James, Estate
Glenn, James, merch [an]t
Graham, Charles
Graham, Jno [John], Estate
Grey, Conrod
Groves, Jonathan
Gunn, Henry

Hall, John
Hall, Moses
Hall, Peter
Hall, Thomas
Hambly, Rich[ar]d
Hamilton, James
Hannah, John
Harris, James
Hawthorn, Jno. [John], Estate
Hearshy, Isaac
Hill, Joseph
Hillis, Geo[rge], Estate
Howell, Lewis, Estate
Hozier, John

Israel, Joseph

Jacquet, Jesse
Jacquet, Paul
Janvier, Joseph
Jones, Enoch, Estate
Jordon, John, Estate

Kerr, Andrew
Kerr, James
Kinkead, Joseph
Kirkpatrick, David

Latimer, ———, Mr., Estate
LeMaigres, Peter, Estate
Leuden, Jno. [John], Estate
Lewis, Isaiah, Estate
Lewis, Joel
Loughery, John
Lownes, Stater
Lyon, John

McBeath, Alex[ande]r
McCallmont, James
McClanahan, Blair, Estate
McClay, William
McCoy, John
McCoy, Nath[anie]l
McCoy, Rob[er]t
McCracken, Hugh
McCracken, James
McCreary, Thomas

McEntier, John
McEntier, Rob[er]t, Estate
McEntier, William
McEntire, Sam[ue]l
McKean, Tho[ma]s, Esq., Estate
McKean, William, Estate
McKonky, David
McMehen, David
McMehen, Margaret
McMehen, William, Esq.
McPhartridge, Malcolmn, Estate
McSparran, Elijah
McSparran, W[illia]m
Magee, James
Martin, John
Martin, William
Mason, Arthur
Maxwell, Solomon
Meanough, Owen
Miller, Isaac, Estate
Montgomery, Rob[er]t, minor, Estate
Montgomery, Tho[ma]s, Estate
Moody, David
Morrison, David
Morrisson, Rob[er]t
Morton, Thomas
Murphy, John
Murphy, William

Nelson, John
Nixon, ———, Mr., Estate

Ogle, Benjamin
Ogle, James
Ogle, Joseph

Palmer, John, Estate
Patten, Matthew, Estate
Patterson, Andrew
Patterson, Will[ia]m
Peery, Jared
Perry, Thomas
Pierce, Isaac, Estate
Platt, John
Platt, Sam[ue]l, Jr.
Platt, Samuel, Sr.
Popham, James
Porter, Robert, Estate
Pratt, George
Price, Mary
Pritchard, Jacob, Estate
Pritchard, John
Pritchard, Joseph

Rankin, Joseph
Rankin, Thomas

Read, James, Estate (Port Penn)
Read, James, Jr., Estate
Read, Tho[ma]s, Estate
Reece, Lewis
Reynolds, Geo[rge]
Rice, Jane
Rink, Sebastian
Roach, Edw[ar]d
Robinson, Jno. [John]
Robinson, Thomas
Robinson, William, and Estate
Rodmon, Phillip
Rogers, Rob[er]t
Rotheram, Joseph
Russel, Geo[rge]
Rutherford, Agness, Estate

Sanky, Geo[rge]
Scott, William, Jr., Estate
Sergeant, John
Sergeant, Obadiah
Shields, Rob[er]t, Estate
Simonton, John
Simpson, Benj[ami]n
Simpson, James
Simpson, William
Slack, Uriah
Slator, John, Estate
Smith, Andrew
Sorrel, Isaac
Sprag, John
Springer, John
Steel, Alex[ande]r, Estate
Steel, Allen, Jr.
Steel, Allen, Sr.
Steel, John, and Estate
Stewart, James, Sr.
Stewart, John, Estate
Stoops, John

Thomas, Isaac, Estate
Thomas, Rich[ar]d, Estate

Wallace, Rob[er]t
Warnock, William
Watkins, Joseph
Watson, Jno. [John], Estate
Welsh, Sylvester
Wilday, John, Estate
Williams, James
Wilson, Jacob, Estate
Wilson, James, Jr.
Wilson, James, Sr.
Wilson, Sam[ue]l, Estate
Woodnot, William

KENT COUNTY
DOVER HUNDRED

Barber, John
Bennet, Benj[ami]n
Bennet, James
Brady, John
Brown, Jonathan
Brown, Thomas
Burns, William
Clark, Ezekiel L[an]d
Clark, Mascle
Cliff, Joseph
Collier, James
Combs, John
Concealer, Thomas
Cooper, George
Craig, [William]
Daugherty, Charles
Denny, Thomas
Dickerson [Dickinson], John, Esq.
Dickerson, John, Jr.
Dixson, George
Down, Henry, Jr.
Duly, Joseph
Durham, Benj[ami]n
Durham, Daniel
Emory, Thomas
Eyler, James
Faris, John
Fisher, Thomas
Foreman, John
Gano, Lewis
Garland, Benj[ami]n
Garner, William
Goforth, George, Jr.
Gordon, James
Gordon, Joshua
Gordon, Sarah
Graham, James
Graham, John
Graham, Robert
Graham, William
Hanson, Samuel
Hart, John
Hood, John
Howell, John
Humpres, George
Irons, Mark
Jackson, Ebenezer
Jackson, Thomas
Jackson, Thomas L[an]d
Jones, James
Jones, Lewis
Knight, Caesar
Lafferty, James

Laws, Outen
Lee, John
Lewis, Stephen (minor)
Linch, John
Lockerman, Mary
Lofland, Purnel
McCaleb, John
McMullen, James
Manlove, Asa
Marim, Charles (minor)
Marim, John
Merideth, Asa
Mifflin, Dary
Miller, John, Rev. L[an]d
Miller, Willin
Mills, Joseph
Muncey, Thomas
Needham, Jonathan
Nickerson, John
Nicols, Vincent
Paradee, Caleb
Paradee, Stephen
Parker, Thomas
Patton, John
Pemberton, James
Pleasanton, David
Pleasanton, John
Pleasanton, Jonathan
Polin, Jonathan
Ratledge, William
Reece, John
Robinson, John
Ross, John
Rowan, John
Rowland, Samuel
Ryans, John
Shay, Elizabeth
Sheohan, John
Sheohan, Jonothon
Slaughter, David
Slaughter, David, Jr.
Slaughter, David, Jr.
Smith, David
Smith, James
Smith, Rich[ar]d L[an]d
Start, Elijah
Start, James
Stephens, Francis
Stephens, James
Stephens, John
Sykes, Ja[me]s L[an]d
Taylor, Joseph
Thomas, Benj[ami]n

Thomas, Moses
Torbert, Hugh
Vanpelt, George
Vanpelt, Joseph
Voshall, John
Wallace, James
Ware, William

Ware, William, Jr.
Watts, William
Weatherhead, John
White, James
White, William
Wilkerson, William
Willy, Waitman

FREE NEGROES

Sipple's Peter
Sipple's Fall
Cook, Peter
Needham's Ack
Tilman, Minso
Moleston's Daniel
Hillyard's Scot
York Derro
Dickerson's Nathan
York Heirs
Hanson's Moses
Dickerson's Pomp, Jr.

Passway, John
Rutther, James
Black, Boslaney
Dickson's Abraham
Richmond's Trusty
Richmond's Omearica
Patten, Peter
Digets, William
Benett, William
Bucher, James
Mearico, Cato

LITTLE CREEK HUNDRED

Allee, Abraham
Allee, Jacob
Alston, Israel
Alston, Thomas (minor)
Amor, John
Arthers, William
Ayres, Simon
Baley, Isaac
Baley, James
Barcus, James
Barcus, Stephen
Barnet, Moses
Barnet, Thomas
Barns, Nathan
Battle, James
Belch, Joseph, Jr.
Bell, Henry
Bell, John L[an]d
Bellach, James, Esq.
Blackshere, Morgan (minor)
Blackshere, Randol
Blackshere, Robert (minor)
Blundel, James
Bradley, Joseph
Bradley, Nathan
Brinkley, Peter
Brison, Charles
Brown, Tho[ma]s (miller)
Buck, Geo[rge]
Buck, Wilson

Buckingham, Isaac (minor)
Burch, Timothy
Burriss, Elisha
Bush, Joseph
Butcher, Robert
Butcher, Thomas, N[egro]
Cahoon, Mark
Caldwell, John
Calwell, Andrew (B)
Chaddock, Charles
Chance, Alexander
Chance, Elijah (minor)
Clark, Freeman
Clark, John, Jr.
Clark, Nicholas
Clark, William
Clark, W[illia]m (in the forest)
Clark, Zadock
Cloake, Samuel
Cloake, Thomas
Collins, John
Cook, William L[an]d
Corse, Thomas L[an]d
Corse, William, Sr. (minor)
Coudratt, Bard
Cowgell, Ezekiel
Cowgell, Daniel
Cowgell, Henry
Cowgell, John, Estate

Cowgell, John, Jr.
Craig, Moses
Crippen, Joseph
Crockett, John
Crockett, Jonathan
Crosley, William
Cross, John
David, Joseph
David, Joseph, Jr.
David, William
Deal, John
Dean, James, N[egro]
Dean, Thomas, N[egro]
Denny, Christopher
Denny, Joseph
Drew, William
Driskill, Joseph
Durberow, Hugh
Durborow, Dan [ie]l L[an]d
Durham, Charles, N[egro]
Durham, Isaiah, N[egro]
Durham, John, N[egro]
Durham, Thomas, N[egro]
Durham, Whitington, N[egro]
Durham, William, N[egro]
Eddenfield, John
Edwards, William
Emerson, Jacob, [Estate]
Emerson, Jonathan
Emerson, Manlove
Everston, Jacob, N[egro]
Fields, Joseph
Flowers, William
Francis, John
Francis, Joseph
Frazer, Alice
Frazer, George
Frazer, John
Frazer, William L[an]d
Garland, John C.
Garrell, Robert
Goodwin, Samuel
Graham, Andrew
Gray, William
Ham, John
Harmon, James, N[egro]
Harper, William
Hatfield, Joseph
Hazell, Isaac
Hickey, John
Hickey, Thomas (minor)
Hill, John
Hines, John
Hirons, William, Jr.
Holston, Richard

Hopkins, Robert
Horn, Robert
Husband, John
Huse, John N[egro]
Hynson, James L[an]d
Jenkens, Jabus
Jenkens, Samuel
Jestis, John
Johnson, John, N[egro]
Jones, Bell
Keith, Francis
Keith, Luke
Keith, Thomas
Kelly, Andrew
Killen, Henry (minor)
Kirkley, George
Kirkley, James
Knotts, William
Lamb, Thomas
Larwood, John
Legg, George
Legg, James
Legg, Samuel
Legg, William
Levick, John (bricklayer)
Levick, William
Lewis, Philip
Logan, David
Longfellow, Thomas
McComb, Eleazer, Esq.
McCoy, Alexander
McCoy, Andrew
McDonald, Joseph
Manlove, Mark
Mattix, William
Maxwell, Samuel L[an]d
Mercer, Benjamin
Mercer, Margarett L[an]d
Merritt, John
Miers, James
Millis, John
Mitchel, William
More, Abraham
Morgan, David
Morgan, Jesse
Needham, Agatha
Newnam, Daniel W.
Nickerson, Lambert
Nock, Daniel
Noudine [Naudain], Andrew
Numbers, Jean
Osburn, Unice
Owens, Ammon
Owens, Rob[er]t
Palmer, John

Parker, Thomas
Parker, Thomas (minor)
Pearson, . . ., widow [of Robert]
Pell, David, Jr.
Penington, William
Poolman, John, N[egro]
Porter, Benjamin
Price, Joseph
Price, Joseph, Jr.
Price, Samuel
Puckam, George
Quilling, Daniel
Rees, Jeremiah, Jr.
Rees, John
Rees, Thomas L[an]d
Ridgaway, James, Jr.
Roach, John
Roalph, Tho[ma]s
Robinson, Antony, N[egro]
Robinson, Charles
Roe, Sam[ue]l, Rev.
Ruth, William
Ryan, Charles
Ryan, John
Scotton, James
Scuce, James
Sears, Stephen
Seliven, Jacob
Seliven, William
Shaw, Henry
Shown, Daniel
Simmons, Gilbert L[an]d
Sisco, Charles, N[egro]
Sisco, Geo[rge], N[egro]
Sisco, John, N[egro]
Sisco, John, Jr., N[egro]
Sisco, John (son of Eph[rai]m)
Smith, William (blacksmith)
Smith, William (son of Richard)

Sowders, John
Standly, Jonas
Stergis, Stoakly (minor)
Sterling, John
Sterling, Mary (widow)
Stevens, Daniel
Stout, Benjamin
Stout, Immanuel (minor)
Stout, Jacob, Esq.
Stout, Mary
Swallow, Joshua
Swany, Timothy
Tanner, David
Tanner, John
Tilghman, Ja[me]s L[an]d
Tilghman, Richard L[an]d
Truett, Boaz
Turley, William
Vanburcalow [Van Burcaloe], Sam[ue]l
Vandergrift, Peter
Vanhoy, Abraham (minor)
Vanhoy, Jacob
Vanstavern, Cornelius
Vanstavern, W[illia]m
Webb, Robert
Wells, Benjamin
Wells, Benjamin, Jr.
Wells, William
Whaley, John
Wharton, Isaiah
Whitman, Samuel minor)
Whittman, Jonathan
Williams, Solomon L[an]d
Williamson, Walter
Wills, Enock
Wood, Aaron
Wright, Solomon L[an]d
Wyn, Benjamin
Wyn, Isaac
Wyn, Simon

FREE NEGROES

Oliver Jackson
Charles Clevor
Ezekiel Whitington
Needham's Ben
Needham's Nathan
Emerson's Ack
Timothy Taught
Zachary Sammons
Negro Mingo
Noxe's Mose
Negro Stepney
Negro Ceasor

Stout's Charles
Jacob Pendergrass
Prince Martain
James Turner
Collins' George
John Collins
John Walker
Peter Frissby
Negro James
Smith's Sam
David Negroe

MISPILLION HUNDRED

Abbitt, James
Accles, Anthoney
Accles, John
Accles, Richard (minor)
Adams, Sarah
Adams, William, Dr.
Allen, Andrew
Allen, John
Anderson, Ezekiel
Anderson, Isaac
Anderson, James
Anderson, Major
Anderson, Rubin
Anderson, William
Argoo, David
Arnitt, William
Artis, [Ro]bart
Artiss, John
Aydelott, Joseph
Barker, [Jam]es
Barker, John
Barker, Joseph
Barker, Thomas, Jr.
Barker, Thomas, Sr.
Barnes, Jesse
Barns, John   M[i]l[for]d
Barwick, Solomon
Bayley, Edward
Baynard, John
Beachampt, David
Beachampt, Macey
Bell, [Robe]rt
Beswick, Curtis
Beswick, George
Beswicks, Vinson
Bidel, Augustine (minor)
Billings, Henry
Black, Benjamin
Black, John, Jr.
Black, [Joh]n, Sr.
Booth, Waitmon
Bostick, [Jaco]b
Bostick, [Ja]mes
Bostick, Major
Bowing, James
Bowing, [Jo]hn
Bowing, William
Bowman, John
Bowman, Nathan
Bowman, Nathaniel, Jr.
Bowman, Nathaniel, Sr.
Bowman, Thomas, Jr.
Bowman, [Willi]am
Boyer, Anthony

Bradford, Isaac
Bradley, William
Brandel, George L[an]d
Bright, Nathan
Brinkley, John, Dr.
Brinkley, Richard L[an]d
Brinkley, William, tanner
Browdy, Robart, Jr.
Browdy, Robart L[an]d
Brown, Betey L[an]d
Brown, George
Brown, [Jam]es
Brown, John, Jr.
Brown, John L[an]d
Brown, William [of] B
Buck, William
Bullock, Thomas
Burriss, Benjamin
Burriss, William
Burrows, William (minor)
Burten, William (minor)
Cain, John
Cain, Othinial
Cain, Thomas, Jr.
Cain, Thomas, Sr.
Calaway, Isaac
Calaway, Jacob
Calaway, John
Calaway, Leven
Calaway, Peter L[an]d
Calaway, William
Caldwell, James
Caldwell, Samuel
Camiel, Jonathan
Canday, William
Cardeen, Daniel
Carman, John
Carmaney, James
Carmean, Jacob
Carmean, Zebdial
Carmon, James
Carmon, John
Carmon, Joseph
Carmon, Thomas
Carpenter, Sarah
Carter, Elias
Carter, Noah
Carter, Samuel
Carvender, Daniel
Case, Charles
Casson, Fardinand
Catlin, Joseph
Catts, James
Catts, Thomas

Catts, Vinson
Catts, William
Chadwick, Thomas
Chahall, Solomon L[an]d
Chahoon, William
Chance, Caleb
Chance, Purnil
Cheesmon, John
Christafer, William
Clark, Benjamin
Clark, Calib
Clark, Henry
Clark, Hugh
Clark, John
Clark, Joshua
Clark, Lott
Clark, Matthew
Clark, Thomas, Jr.
Clark, Thomas [df] Nich[olas]
Clark, William
Clifton, Daniel L[an]d
Clifton, Jehu
Clifton, Manlove
Clifton, Nathan
Clifton, Thomas (minor)
Clifton, Thomas, Jr.
Clifton, Thomas, Sr.
Cole, Richard
Colescoott, John
Collins, Andrew
Collins, John
Collins, John M[i]lf[ord]
Collins, Thomas
Coppage, John
Cordarey, Isaac
Cork, Isaac (minor)
Cork, James
Cox, Gove
Cox, Isaac
Cox, John, B. Sw[amp]
Cox, John, Jr.
Cox, John, Sr.
Cranor, Thomas
Crapper, Leven
Crippen, John
Cromton, John [of] F
Cromton, John M[il]f[or]d
Cullen, John
Cullen, Charles
Culley, Roger
Cullin, Elias
Cullin, Hezekiah
Cullin, Isaac
Cullin, James
Cullin, William

Dalanor, John
Dalanor, Richard
Daley, William
Daughaty, George
Daughaty, George [of] Thomas
Daughaty, John
Davis, Andrew
Davis, Brinkley
Davis, David, cooper
Davis, Henery
Davis, Isaac
Davis, Jehu, Esqr.
Davis, John
Davis, John, sadler
Davis, Mathias
Davis, Robart
Davis, Thomas of Robert
Davis, Thomas
Davis, William of R.
Daws, John
Dawson, Asa
Dawson, John
Dawson, Jonas
Dawson, Zebdeal
Depray, William
Deweast, Thomas
Deweise, Cornelus, Jr.
Deweise, Cornelus, Sr.
Deweise, David
Deweist, Jashua
Dickerson, Henry (minor)
Dill, Abner
Dillen, John L[an]d
Dillin, Ezekiel
Dillin, Nehemiah
Dormon, George
Downs, Benjamin
Draper, Lemuel
Draper, William
Draper, William, Sr.
Drapor, John
Duglas, James
Dunnum, John
Dutten, Thomas
Dwigens, Samuel
Earl, Richard (minor)
Edgin, Benjamin
Edgin, Henery
Edgin, William
Eliott, Edward
Eliott, Thomas
Elliss, Jessey
Estil, William
Evens, William
Fairbanks, William
Finchwait, James

Finchwait, Jonathan
Finchwait, Jonathan, Jr.
Finchwait, Thomas
Fisher, Abraham
Fisher, Edward
Fisher, Henery
Fisher, Jabiz
Fisher, James, Jr.
Fisher, James M[arshy] Hope
Fi[sher], John
Fisher, John, Sr.
Fisher, Richard
Fisher, William
Flamor, John (malot. [mulato])
Fleming, . . . (widow of W[illia]m)
Fleming, Archable (minor)
Fleming, Beniah
Fleming, George
Fleming, James (of R.)
Fleming, Joseph
Fleming, Robart
Fleming, Samuel
Folks, Daniel L[an]d (minor)
Fossett, Smith
Founting, John
Frazer, William
Frelin, Levy
Gannon, John
Garrell, Stephen L[an]d
Gaskins, William
Gerrill, [Ja]mes
Glandon, Thomas
Glass, Bilotha
Glazer, [Da]vid
Godwin, Daniel
Godwin, Ezekiel
Godwin, [Jam]es
Godwin, John
Godwin, Joseph
Godwin, Kimmiel (minor)
Godwin, Nahor
Godwin, Preston
Godwin, Thomas
Godwin, William
Goldsbuross, Robart (minor)
Goore, [Ge]orge
Goslee, Samuel
Goslin, Samuel L[an]d
Grayham, [Geor]ge, Jr.
Grayham, Isreal
Grayham, John
Grayham, Samuel
Grayhanes, George
Griffith, Henry
Griffith, Isaac
Griffith, [Ja]mes

Griffith, John
Grissom, Christerfer
Gullett, Abraham
Gullett, George
Gullett, Isaac
Gullett, John
Gullett, Joshua
Hadox, Isaac
Hall, William
Hall, Winlock
Hambleton, Hosa
Hambleton, James
Hambleton, Joel
Hambleton, John, Jr.
Hardestee, James
Hardistee, William (minor)
Harington, Aaron
Harington, Absolum
Harington, Barsha
Harington, David
Harington, James
Harington, Nathan
Harmon, Middleton
Harmonson, Luke
Harper, Joseph
Harper, William
Harrengton, John L[an]d
Hatfeild, James
Hazlett, Joseph
Hearington, Henry (minor)
Helford, Robart
Helford, Thomas
Helford, Zadock
Henderixson, Samuel
Henderson, James
Henderxson, Jacobees
Hendrickson, Henry
Hevilow, Zadock
Hickmond, Jacob
Hickmond, Jacob, Jr.
Hilmon, Thomas
Hilmon, William
Hopkins, James L[an]d
Hopkins, John, Jr.
Hopkins, John, Sr.
Hopkins, John, Sr. L[an]d
Hopkins, Robart, Jr.
Hopkins, Robert, Sr.
Hopkins, Zabulin
Houston, Elijah L[an]d
Houston, John
Houston, Purniel
Howard, John
Howrin, William
Hudson, William
Hughlett, Thomas (minor)

Hunn, Nathaniel
Jacobs, Bosmon
Jacobs, James
Jacobs, Speakman
Jacobs, William (of Speakman)
Jacobs, William (of W[illia]m)
James, Isaiah
Jester, Abraham
Jester, Elias
Jester, Ely
Jester, Emanuel
Jester, Frances L[an]d
Jester, Frances, Jr.
Jester, Isaac
Jester, John
Jester, John (of F.)
Jester, Lamee
Jester, Thomas
Jester, Thomas
Jester, Jessey
Jones, Curtis
Jones, Isaac
Jones, Leven
Jones, Mathias
Jones, Robart (minor)
Jones, Salathiel
Jones, Stephen
Jonson, James
Jonson, Nathin
Jonson, Samuel
Jonson, Thomas
Jonson, William   M[i]sp[illion]
Jonson, William   Brs. Neck
Jump, Christerfer
Jump, Leven
Kelley, James
Kelley, William
Kemmey, Leven, Jr.
Kemmey, Robart
Killensworth, Luke
Killing, Able
Killing, Mark
Kimmey, Abraham
Kimmey, Solomon
King, John
King, Peter
Lain, Anthoney
Lain, James
Lansley, George
Lansley, Isaac
Latchampt, George
Latchampt, Peter
Laws, Belitha (minor)
Laws, Joshua
Laws, Leah
Laws, Major

Laws, William
Layrea, James
Layton, James
Leadenhem, Zadock
Leaventon, Richard
Leaverton, Gary
Lecompt, Nathan
Lewis, Stephen, Esq.
Listen, James
Lister, Peter
Lister, William, Jr.
Lister, William, Sr.
Lockwood, Isaac
Lodwick, Jacob
Lofland, Solomon
Lowber, Isaac
Lowber, Peter
Luff, Calib
Luff, Nathaniel, Sr.
McGonnagal, Robart
McKnett, John (of Ja[me]s)
McKnett, Robart
McNatt, Daniel
McNatt, John, Jr.
McNatt, Joseph
McNatt, Major
McNatt, William, Jr.
McNatt, William, Sr.
McNatt, William (of W[illia]m)
McNett, James
Madden, Elisha
Majous, John L[an]d
Manlove, George
Manlove, Jonathan
Manlove, Mathew
Marress, Elijah
Marrett, Abel (of Sam.)
Marrett, John
Marrett, Joseph
Marrett, Samuel
Masey, Ezekiel
Mason, Charles
Mason, Elias
Mason, Isaac
Mason, Jacob
Mason, John
Mason, Joseph
Masten, Hezekiah
Masten, John, Jr.
Masten, John, Sr.
Masten, Mathias, Jr.
Masten, Mathias, Sr.
Masten, William, Jr.
Masten, William, Sr.
Mearadith, Joshua
Mearadith, Samuel

Mearadith, William
Middleton, Absolum
Miffen, Mathew
Miffen, William
Mills, Clifton
Milven, Barthalumu
Milven, David
Milven, Edward
Milven, George
Milven, James
Milven, John
Milven, Jonathan
Milven, Joshua
Milvin, Solomon
Minies, Robart
Minner, Stephen
Minner, Thomas
Molleston, Jonathan (minor)
Molliston, Henery
Morgan, Even
Morgan, James
Morgan, Robart (minor)
Morgan, William
Morgin, Peter   Milf[or]d
Moriss, Noah
Morphy, Levin
Morress, Cornelus
Morress, Dickerson
Morress, Elisha
Morress, Jeremiah   L[an]d
Morress, John
Morress, John (son of James)
Morress, Levy
Morress, Samuel
Morress, Samuel, Jr.
Morress, Samuel (of Jos[eph])
Morress, William
Morresse, Elijah
Morriss, John, carpenter
Murphey, Elijah
Murphey, John, Jr.
Murphey, John, Sr.
Murphey, William
Murphey, William (of John)
Needles, Henry   L[an]d
Needles, John
Needles, William
Nickerson, Joshua
Noliston, Samuel
Nowell, Edward
Nowell, Jehu
Nowell, Samuel
Nuckum, John
Nutter, James
Oliver, Gilladitt
Oliver, Joseph, Esq.

Oliver, Joseph, Jr.
Painter, James
Paritt, Joseph
Parker, James
Parker, John
Parson, John, Jr.
Parson, John, Sr.
Patten, Andrew
Peag, John
Ptarce, David
Pearce, Joseph
Peasley, [Sam]uel
Pennawell, Elijah
Peterkin, David
Pettegreu, John
Pindergrass, Patrick
Pitts, William
Pleasenton, John
Pleasenton, Margett,   L[an]d
Porter, John
Potter, Benjamin
Powell, Price
Powell, Samuel
Powell, William
Powell, Zadock
Pratt, George
Price, John
Primrose, John
Primrose, Thomas
Pritchett, Ezeakel, Sr.
Pritchett, Ezekiel, Jr.
Pritchett, Zachariah
Purden, James (minor)
Ralley, Thomas
Ralstone, John, Esq.
Rannells, William
Rathal, Thomas
Rayfeild, Peter
Reed, Ezekiel
Reed, James
Reed, John, Jr.
Reed, John, Sr.
Reed, Thomas
Reed, William
Reed, William (B.   Sw[am]p)
Regerster, James
Regley, Benjamin
Reson, Benjamin (minor)
Revel, John, Esq.
Richardson, Abraham
Rickards, John
Ridgway, Nathan
Riggs, Esaiah
Riggs, Ezekiel
Robeson, Joseph   Milford
Roland, David

Roland, Jonathan   L[an]d
Ross, Thomas
Rotten, Henry
Rotten, James
Rotten, William   L[an]d
Russom, Peter
Russum, William
Sapp, Jacob
Saterfeild, Broffett
Satterfield, Aaron
Satterfield, Joseph
Satterfield, Nathaniel
Saulsbury, William   L[an]d
Saxson, George
Saxson, William (of W[illia]m)
Saxson, William, Sr.
Scoott, Ebenezer
Scoott, John
Scoott, John, Sr.
Scoott, Nathan
Scoott, William
Seppel, Elijah (minor)
Shepperd, Thomas (minor)
Shockley, Davis
Shockley, Elias
Shockley, Thomas
Simson, John
Simson, Robart
Simson, Thomas
Sippel, Boot
Sippel, Calib   L[an]d
Sippel, Silva
Sippel, Thomas
Sippel, Zadek
Slaughter, John
Slaughter, Jonathan   L[an]d
Smethers, Nathaniel
Smith, Benjamin
Smith, Bentin
Smith, Charls
Smith, Daniel (of Daniel)
Smith, Daniel, Sr.
Smith, David
Smith, Holaday
Smith, James
Smith, James
Smith, John
Smith, Ralph
Smith, Robert
Smith, Thomas (of Daniel)
Smith, Thomas (of Jester)
Smith, Thomas (of Thomas)
Smith, Thomas, Sr.
Smith, William (of Daniel)
Soden, Anna Reter
Soden, James (minor)

Soden, Thomas
Soden, William
Soute, Jacob
Spencer, Joshua
Spencer, Samuel
Stafford, John
Start, Richerd
Stashey, Leven
Stephens, George (minor)
Stirgis, William
Stokes, Lemuel
Stradley, Abraham
Stradley, Calib
Stradley, Thomas
Stradley, Zadock
Stroud, Thomas
Stuart, Andrew (minor)
Stuart, George
Stuart, John
Swiggett, Henry (minor)
Tamplin, Isaac
Tatnil, William (minor)
Taylor, Jenifer, Esq.
Taylor, John
Taylor, John, Jr. F
Taylor, John   M[i]lf[ord]
Taylor, Peter
Taylor, Stephen
Taylor, Walter
Taylor, William
Tharp, William
Tharp, William   L[an]d
Thislewood, Daniel
Thislewood, Emanuel
Thislewood, James
Thislewood, John
Thislewood, William
Thislewood, William (of W[illia]m)
Thomas, Daniel
Thomas, James, Jr.
Thomas, John
Thomas, Thomas
Thomas, Thomas (N R)
Thomas, Thomas, Sr.
Thomson, William, Jr.
Thomson, William, Sr.
Thorn, Sydenham, Revd.   L[an]d
Thownsand, Solomon
Tolson, Alexander
Townsand, Charles
Townsand, John
Travise, Matthew   L[an]d
Trippett, Gove
Truett, George
Tucker, David
Tucker, John, Sr.

Tucker, Shadrick
Tumbelston, Richard
Tumbelston, Tho[ma]s L[an]d
Tumbelston, Thomas, Jr.
Tumbelstone, Cary
Tumbleston, Tho[ma]s
Tumblin, Covel L[an]d
Turner, Benjamin
Turner, Charles
Turner, George
Turner, Jehu
Turner, Samuel B.
Vain, Thomas
Vaulx, William
Viccory, John
Viccory, Thomas
Viccory, Waitmon
Vinson, Daniel
Vinson, Eliab L[an]d
Vinson, James
Vinson, Jessee
Vinson, Jethru
Virden, Absolum (minor)
Virdin, John
Walker, John
Walton, . . . (widow)
Ward, Joseph
Ward, Richard
Ward, William
Watson, John
Webb, John
Webster, Thomas
Wheatley, William (minor)
Whitaker, James
White, Edward (of Edw[ard])
White, Edward, Esq.
White, Thomas, Jr.
White, William
Whitehead, Jacob
Whitehead, Lemuel
Wiatt, Aaron
Wiatt, John
Wiatt, Moses
Wiatt, Solomon
Wiatt, Thomas
Wilcutt, . . . (widow)
Wilcutt, Calib
Wilcutt, Leven
Wilegoos, Thomas B.
Willcutts, William
Willey, Gabril L[an]d
Willey, Leven
William, John (Stuart)
William, Thomas

Williams, Aaron
Williams, Charles
Williams, Daniel L[an]d
Williams, James
Williams, John
Williams, John, Sr.
Williams, Rineor
Williams, Ward
Willour, John
Willour, Thomas
Wilson, Elizabeth
Wilson, James
Wilson, Robart L[an]d
Wings, . . . (widow) L[an]d (minor)
Winsmore, Thomas
Woters, Elijah (minor)
Yoe, Benjamin
Young, Benjamin
Young, David

FREE NEGROES

Lewises Cessor
Abraham Bell
Lawes Jacob
Fisher Guy
Sodens Dover
Caldwells Saul
Doto Charles
Sipples Tobe
White Raddy
Barwick Silous
Peterkins Peter
Dewests Cuff
James Price or Scott
Maxwell Isaac
Rogeres Jacob
Henry Van
Bradley Jess
Taylor Abraham
Crapper Lundon
Irons Cook
Manlove Pomp
Mifflins James
Spencers Harklus
Draper John
Manlove George
Mollenstons Robart
Irons Steave
Sipples Daniel
Woodcook Absolam
Revils Henery
Spencers Jacob

MURDERKILL HUNDRED

Aaron, David
Abbit, Thomas
Alford, Joseph
Alford, Maccabee
Alford, W[illia]m L[an]d
Allaband, Tho[ma]s
Allaband, William
Allen, Charles
Alston, Stephen
Amos, George
Amos, James
Amos, John
Anderson, Andrew
Anderson, Andrew (Cox)
Anderson, Bartholomew
Anderson, Clothier
Anderson, John
Anderson, William
Argadine, Mark
Argadine, William

Baily, Geo[rge]
Banning, John, Esq.
Banning, Phenias
Banning, Rich[ar]d
Barber, Abram (minor of)
Barber, Francis
Barber, Joseph
Barcus, Tho[ma]s
Barker, Abner
Barker, Joseph
Barker, Tho[ma]s
Barker, William
Barratt, And[re]w, Esq.
Barratt, Elijah
Barratt, Philip
Barry, Ja[me]s
Bartlet, John
Bassett, Rich[ar]d, Esq.
Bateman, Geo[rge]
Battell, Elizabeth
Battell, French
Battell, French (minor)
Battell, John
Beauchamp, Costen
Beauchamp, Jereboam
Beauchamp, Joshua
Beauchamp, Levi
Beauchamp, Newell
Bedwell, Geo[rge]
Bedwell, Ja[me]s (Johnson)
Bedwell, Preston
Bedwell, Tho[ma]s
Bedwell, Tho[ma]s, Jr.
Beer, Isaac

Beer, W[illia]m
Bell, John
Bell, John, Jr.
Bennet, Angelo
Bennet, John
Berry, Benja[min]
Berry, Cha[rle]s
Berry, Elijah
Berry, Ja[me]s
Berry, Joseph
Berry, Tho[ma]s
Berry, William
Berry, W[illia]m, merc[han]t
Birt, Elsebury
Birt, Henry L[an]d
Birt, John L[and]d
Bishop, Will[ia]m
Black, Stephen (minor of)
Black, W[illia]m
Blackshare, Miriam
Blizard, John
Body, Philip
Boggs, Joseph L[an]d
Boon, ... (Slaughter's Land.)
Boon, Moses L[an]d
Boor, Perry
Bostick, John
Bostick, William
Bowers, John
Bowers, Rachel
Bowman, Tho[ma]s
Boyd, W[illia]m
Boyer, Caleb L[an]d
Boyer, Cha[rle]s
Boyer, Dan[ie]l
Boyer, Will[ia]m
Bradley, John
Brady, Benja[min]
Brice, Benedict L[an]d
Bright, Nathan
Broadway, Ambross (minor of)
Broadway, Sam[ue]l
Broadway, W[illia]m L[an]d
Brooks, Arthur
Broom, Jacob
Brown, Benja[min] (minor of)
Brown, John
Brown, John (Rich[ard])
Brown, John (Voshal)
Brown, Rachel
Brown, Severson
Brown, Tho[ma]s (Noah)
Brown, Tho[ma]s, carp[en]t[er]
Brown, William (Dover)

Brummel, Jacob
Bryan, Tho[ma]s
Buckley, Arnold
Buckmaster, John
Buckmaster, Tho[ma]s
Bullock, . . . (widow)
Bullock, Ezekiel (minor)
Burchinel, Jeremiah, Jr.
Burchinel, Joseph (minor)
Burchman, John
Butler, Elizabeth
Butler, John
Butler, Will[ia]m

Cahoon, John
Cain, Francis
Calbreth, W[illia]m
Caldwell, John
Caldwell, Timothy
Caldwell, Train
Callaghan, Edward
Carlisle, Tho[ma]s
Carpenter, . . ., Doctor
Carpenter, W[illia]m (heirs)
Carter, Daniel
Carter, Edward (minor)
Carter, Geo[rge]
Carter, Henry
Carter, Mary
Cass, John
Casson, Mire
Caton, Benjamin
Caton, John
Catts, Tho[ma]s
Chairs, John
Chairs, Tho[ma]s
Chambers, . . . (widow)
Chambers, John
Chambers, John, weaver
Chambers, Joseph (minor)
Chapman, Samual
Chipman, Stephen
Chipman, Tho[ma]s (Land)
Chippy, Joshua
Clark, . . . (widow)
Clark, Absalom
Clark, Absalom, Jr.
Clark, John
Clark, Lemuel
Clark, Rob[er]t
Clark, Sam[ue]l
Clark, Vincent
Clark, W[illia]m (Cox)
Clayton, Ja[me]s
Clayton, John, Esq.
Clifton, Matthias
Clymer, Cha[rle]s

Clymer, Massy
Cohea, Benjamin
Cohea, Lemuel
Coleman, Ja[me]s
Collins, Isaac
Collins, Johnson
Colter, Eli
Conceler, John
Conner, John
Conner, Samuel
Conner, Solomon
Cook, Daniel (Campden)
Cook, Risdon
Coomb, Benjamin, Esq.
Coomb, Griffith
Coomb, John
Cooper, George
Cooper, Geor[ge], Jr.
Cooper, John
Cooper, Richard, Esq.
Corker, John
Corse, John
Countis, Peter
Covey, Francis
Cox, Dan[ie]l
Cox, Isaac
Cox, Matthew
Craige, . . . (widow)
Craige, Ja[me]s (minor)
Craige, John
Craige, Samuel
Craige, Samuel (minor)
Cramner, Geo[rge]
Cramner, Tho[ma]s
Cramner, Tho[ma]s (minor of)
Crane, Patrick
Crooks, Benjamin
Crumpton, Curtis
Cubbage, George
Cubbage, John
Cubbage, Philemon
Cubbage, Tho[ma]s
Culley, Ja[me]s
Cummings, Daniel
Cummings, Joshua

Davis, Benjamin
Davis, Isaac
Davis, James
Davis, John (Manrings)
Davis, Thomas
Daws, William
Daws, William, Jr.
Dawson, Shadrach
Deal, John
Derrick, George
Derrick, Richard

Dewese, Elijah
Dewese, Isaac
Dewese, Samuel
Dill, Benjamin
Dill, Jacob
Dill, John (Oldfield)
Dill, John, Esq.
Dill, John W.
Dill, Philemon
Dill, Solomon
Dill, Solomon, Jr.
Dill, Thomas
Dill, Vincent
Dill, William
Dixon, Jessee
Dixon, Rob[er]t L[an]d
Dixon, Thomas
Dolby, William
Dolman, George
Dorrel, James
Dougherty, Vincent
Dougle, King
Downham, Isaac
Downham, Joseph
Downham, Richard
Downham, Thomas
Downs, ... (widow) L[an]d
Downs, Stephen
Downs, Stephen, Jr.
Downs, William
Draper, Isaac L[an]d
Dudley, Nicholas
Duhadaway, Jacob
Dunning, Samuel
Dunning, Tho[ma]s
Dunning, Willia m
Dupoister, Tho[ma]s
Durborow, ... (widow)
Dyal, Robert
Dyer, ... (widow)
Dyer, Joseph

Edmonds, John
Edmondson, Emanuel L[an]d
Edmondson, Francis (heirs)
Edmondson, John
Edmondson, Joseph L[an]d
Edmondson, Joshua
Edmondson, Thomas
Elbert, Joshua L[an]d
Elliott, James
Emmerson, Jacob
Emmerson, Jon[atha]n (heirs)
Emmerson, Vincent L[an]d
Emmery, Arthur
Emmery, Charles
Emmery, John (forest)

Emmery, John R.
Emmery, Tho[ma]s
Emmery, W[illia]m
Ennald, Henry (Lot)
Errickson, Jacob
Ethards, And[re]w
Ethards, Phil
Farmer, John
Farmer, W[illia]m, Jr.
Fisher, John
Fisher, John L[an]d
Fisher, Joshua, Esq.
Folk, Samuel
Folk, Thomas
Ford, Daniel
Ford, John
Ford, Thomas
Foreacre, Rob[er]t
Fowler, John
Frazier, James
Frazier, W[illia]m
Freeman, Asa
Freeman, John
French, George
Furbee, Caleb
Furbee, Esther
Furbee, Jacob
Furbee, Jo[nat]h[a]n (minor)
Furbee, Michael
Furtad, Joseph

George, James
George, John
George, Joseph
George, Tho[ma]s
Gibbs, Benjamin L[an]d
Gilder, Henry L[an]d
Gilder, John
Gildersleve, George
Gildersleve, John
Gildersleve, Jon[atha]n
Gisford, James
Goforth, George
Goforth, John
Goforth, Peter
Goldsborow, John L[an]d
Golt, Elijah
Golt, George
Gooden, John
Gooden, Moses
Gordon, John, Esq.
Gordon, Seth
Gray, David
Gray, John
Gray, W[illia]m
Gray, W[illia]m (Dill)

Gray, W[illia]m (of David)
Green, James
Green, John
Green, Thomas   L[an]d
Green, W[illia]m
Greenly, David
Greenly, James
Greenly, Rob[er]t
Grewell, Jacob
Grewell, John
Grier, John
Grier, John, Jr.
Guy, W[illia]m

Hadabough, Abram
Hadabough, Isaac
Hadabough, Warwick
Hairgrove, George
Hairgrove, John
Hairgrove, Stephen
Hale, Joseph
Halee, Joseph, Jr.
Hanson, Samuel
Hanson, Timothy
Hardcastle, Dater
Harper, David, Jr.
Harper, John
Harper, Joseph
Harper, Thomas
Harrington, Samuel
Harris, Abram
Hartshorn, John
Harwood, John
Harwood, Peter
Harwood, Samuel (minor)
Harwood, Thomas
Hatfield, John
Hatfield, Levi
Hatfield, Levin
Hatfield, W[illia]m
Hatfield, William, Sr.
Hazelton, W[illia]m
Heald, John (heirs)
Hendrickson, W[illia]m
Hernsley, W[illia]m   L[an]d
Herrington, Gideon
Herrington, Isaac
Herrington, Jacob
Herrington, Nathan
Hillyard, Charles
Hindsley, Ambrose
Hindsley, Amos
Hindsley, Garret
Hindsley, James
Hindsley, Nathan
Hinman, Baily
Hobson, John

Hobson, W[illia]m
Hodgson, Joseph
Hodgson, Rob[er]t
Holland, Abram
Homestead, Jon[atha]n
Horn, George
Horton, Christopher
Howard, John
Howard, W[illia]m
Howell, Samuel
Howell, W[illia]m
Hudson, John
Huff, Nathan
Hunn, Jon[atha]n
Hunn, Jon[atha]n, Jr.
Hurlock, ... (widow)
Huston, ... (widow)
Huston, Alex[ande]r (minor)
Hutchins, ames   L[an]d
Hutson, Alex[ande]r
Hutson, James

Ireland, William   L[an]d
Irons, Henry
Irons, Timothy

Jackson, Alex[ander]
Jackson, Daniel
Jackson, Ezekiel
Jackson, George   L[an]d
Jackson, John
Jackson, Jon[atha]n
Jackson, Joseph (Emry)
Jackson, Joseph (minor)
Jackson, Moses
Jackson, Thomas
Jackson, Thomas, carp[en]t[er]
James, Daniel
Jarratt, Matthew
Jarvis, Caleb
Jarvis, Joseph
Jerrald, Elias
Jerrald, Hart
Jerrald, Ja[me]s
Jerrald, Jerre
Jerrald, Jona[than]
Jerrald, Rob[er]t
Jinkins, Jabez
Jinkins, Thomas
Johnson, James
Johnson, John
Johnson, John, Jr.
Johnson, W[illia]m
Jones, Benja[min]   L[an]d
Jones, Daniel
Jones, David
Jones, Garret

Jones, Jacob
Jones, Jacob, Doctor
Jones, James
Jones, James (Pierce)
Jones, Jesse
Jones, John
Jones, Moses
Jones, Phip
Jones, W[illia]m
Jump, Solomon

Kees, John
Kees, W[illia]m
Kersey, Moses
Killen, Jacob
Killen, John
Killen, William, Esq.
Killen, W[illia]m, Jr.
Kilpatrick, John
Kimmy, Joseph
Kirkley, Thomas
Kirkley, William

Lamden, Daniel
Lamden, John
Lard, Henry
Latcham, Isaiah
Lee, Thomas
Lemar, Benjamin
Lemar, Gallent
Lewis, David
Lewis, Evan
Lewis, John
Lewis, Joseph
Lewis, Rob[er]t
Lewis, Thomas
Lockwood, Armwell
Lockwood, Armwell, Jr.
Lockwood, John
Lockwood, Thomas
Lofland, Isaac
Loftis, Burton
Loftis, Gideon
Loftis, John
Loftis, Joseph
Longfellow, John
Loockerman, Betsy
Loockerman, Nicho[la]s
Lowber, Daniel
Lowber, Daniel, saddler
Lowber, John
Lowber, Jonathan
Lowber, Mathew
Lowber, Peter
Lowber, Peter, tanner
Lowber, W[illia]m
Lucas, James

Lucas, Mason
Luff, Nath[anie]l
Lundergill, James
Lynn, John

McBride, Morris
McBride, Rob[er]t
McBride, Samuel
McCall, George
McCall, Mark
McClement, James, Esq.
McClement, Robert
McClement, Unity
McClement, W[illia]m
McEver, James
McEver, Timothy
McGarmont, Mary
McGifford, John
McGinnes, Charles
McPherson, Hugh
Magaw, Samuel L[an]d
Manlove, George
Manlove, Mott L[an]d
Manning, Thomas
Manring, ... (widow)
Manring, Richard
Manring, Richard, Jr.
Mansfield, Edward
Mansfield, W[illia]m
Many, Francis, Esq.
Marker, Curtis
Marker, Timothy
Mason, Richard
Mason, William
Mason, William, Jr.
Maxwell, Bedwell
Maxwell, David
Maxwell, Edmondson
Maxwell, Nimrod
Meredith, Job
Meredith, Job, Jr.
Meredith, Job (of Hook)
Meredith, John
Meredith, Joseph
Meredith, Nathan
Meredith, W[illia]m
Meredith, William, Jr.
Merrick, Israel L[an]d
Middlehouse, John
Mifflin, Daniel
Mifflin, Warner
Milbourn, Samuel
Milbourn, Samuel, Jr.
Miles, James
Miller, Conrod
Miller, Conrod, Jr.
Miller, Edward

Miller, John
Miller, John (of Henry)
Miller, Peter
Millis, James
Milloway, James
Minner, Solomon
Mires, W[illia]m
Mitten, James, Jr.
Moore, Caleb
Moore, George
Moore, Isaac
Moore, John
Moore, Samuel
Moore, W[illia]m
Moore, William, Jr.
Morris, Absalom
Morris, Eliz[abe]th
Morris, Emanuel
Morris, John
Morris, W[illia]m, tanner
Morris, W[illia]m, of tanner
Morris, William (little son)
Mott, Charles
Muncy, ... (widow)
Muncy, John
Muncy, Thomas
Murphy, Charles
Murphy, Jon[atha]n

Needles, Thomas
Needles, W[illia]m
Newell, Henry
Newman, James
Newton, Isaac
Newton, Josiah
Nichols, Moses
Niel, ... (widow)
Niel, James
Niels, Jonathan (minor)
Nixon, Charles
Nock, Joseph
Nock, Thomas
Nolen, Matthew
North, George
North, James

Oldfield, Henry

Parker, W[illia]m
Parker, W[illia]m (warren)
Parvis, Absalom
Parvis, Richard
Parvis, William
Parvis, W[illia]m, Jr.
Patten, W[illia]m
Peirce, Jacob
Peirce, William

Peirce, William (Jocky)
Peirce, William, Jr.
Pemberton, John
Pennell, John (minor)
Pennywell, W[illia]m
Perry, George
Perry, James
P[er]ry, John
Pickring, Thomas
Piper, Spear
Polk, Shavers   L[an]d
Poor, Henry
Potts, John
Powell, John
Powell, William
Pratt, Fredrick
Preston, John
Price, James
Price, John
Price, Matthew
Price, Thomas
Price, Tho[ma]s (of Frank)
Proctor, Thomas (minor)
Pryor, ... (widow)
Pryor, Abram
Purden, Andrew (minor)
Purden, William
Purkins, Thomas
Purnel, Thomas

Quillen, John
Quinley, James

Rash, Andrew
Rash, John
Rash, Joseph
Ratlidge, John
Reed, George
Reed, John
Rees, W[illia]m
Register, Elijah
Register, Francis
Register, Isaac
Register, Jerre
Register, Rob[er]t
Rench, Henry
Reynolds, Alexander   L[an]d
Reynolds, Daniel
Reynolds, Michael
Reynolds, Rob[er]t
Reynolds, Thomas
Rich, Peter
Rich, Stephen
Richards, Henry
Richardson, James
Rickets, Charles
Rickets, Elijah

Rickets, Thomas
Ridgely, Anne
Ridgely, George
Ridgely, Henry
Ridgely, Mary
Ridgely, Nicholas, Esq.
Ridgely, Williamina
Ridgway, Thomas
Roberts, John
Robinson, Alexander　L[an]d
Robinson, James
Robinson, Margaret
Robinson, Samuel
Rodney, Letitia
Rodney, Thomas, Esq.
Roe, Brinckle
Rogers, Edward
Rogers, Joseph
Rogirson, Fidelia
Ross, Peter
Ross, Rob[er]t
Rowan, George
Rowland, Isaiah
Rundel, Daniel　L[an]d
Ryley, W[illia]m, taylor

Sapp, James
Sapp, W[illia]m
Saxton, Alexander
Scotton, Eli
Scotton, Thomas
Scotton, W[illia]m
Seal, Joseph
Seany, Bryon
Shadwick, Samuel
Shaver, ... L[an]d
Shaw, James
Shaw, Joshua　L[an]d
Shaw, W[illia]m　L[an]d
Shehorn, John
Shepperd, Benjamin
Sherwood, John
Silvester, Herrington
Sipple, Caleb
Sipple, Elias
Sipple, Garrett
Sipple, John
Sipple, Silvia
Sipple, Thomas
Sipple, Waitman
Skidmore, Thomas　L[an]d
Skinner, Thomas
Slaughter, Stephen　L[an]d
Slay, Edward
Smack, Kendle
Smack, McKimmy
Smith, Benjamin

Smith, James, merchant
Smith, Jessee
Smith, John　L[an]d
Smith, John (of David)
Smith, John (of James)
Smith, John, Jr.
Smith, Joseph
Smith, Nathaniel
Smith, Richard
Smith, Samuel (of Benjamin)
Smith, Wheeler
Smith, W[illia]m
Smith, W[illia]m (Maxwells)
Smithers, John
Smithers, Joseph
Soward, George
Soward, Thomas
Spencer, Isaiah
Spencer, W[illia]m
Spry, John
Stanton, Joshua
Start, James
Start, John
Staton, Hillah
Stidham, Thomas
Stinson, Ephraim
Stinson, John
Stinson, John (Dover)
Story, Andrew
Stow, John
Stradley, Absalom
Stradley, Caleb
Stradley, David
Stradley, Isaiah
Stradley, Nathaniel
Summers, Nathaniel
Summers, Zael
Sykes, James, Esq.
Sykes, James, Jr.

Taffey, Peter
Taylor, Benjamin
Taylor, Elijah
Taylor, Isaac
Taylor, Major
Taylor, Peter
Taylor, Richard
Taylor, Thomas
Teat, James
Thawley, Edward
Thomas, Benjamin
Thomas, Evan
Thomas, George
Thomas, Thomas, Jr.
Thompson, Cary
Thompson, William
Tilton, James

Tilton, Nehe[mi]a[h]
Tomlin, John
Townsend, Anne
Townsend, Benjamin
Townsend, William
Trigger, Zebedie L[an]d
Trippit, Terril
Truitt, Curtis
Truitt, George, Esq.
Truitt, Henry
Truitt, Solomon
Truitt, Zadock
Tubman, Ananias

Vanattee, Samuel
Vanattie, Thomas
Vanburculo, Peter
Vandiver, Thomas
Vincent, John
Vining, John
Virdin, John
Virdin, Peter
Virdin, William
Voshal, James (of Obed[iah])
Voshal, Obediah

Wainwright, Reuben
Waker, John, cordwainer
Walker, Daniel
Walker, John
Wallace, Jon[atha]n
Wallace, Joseph
Wallace, W[illia]m
Walston, John L[an]d
Walston, Thomas
Walton, Fisher
Walton, George
Walton, George, taylor
Ward, Henry L[an]d
Ward, John
Ward, W[illia]m
Warner, W[illia]m
Warren, Eliz[abe]th
Warren, Haddock
Warren, John
Warren, Lodman
Warren, Samuel
Watson, John
Weahman, James (Lot)
Wells, David
Wheeler, Daniel

Wheeler, John
Wheeler, Lemuel
White, Alexander
White, Jacob
White, John
White, John L[an]d
White, Richard
White, W[illia]m (of Richard)
Whitely, Arthur L[an]d
Wild, Thomas
Wild, William
Wilkinson, Nathan
Wilkinson, Thomas
Wilkinson, Thomas, Jr.
Willaby, Asa
Willaby, Samuel
Williams, Andrew
Williams, Benjamin
Williams, Chris[tophe]r L[an]d
Williams, James
Williams, James (of Benj[amin])
Williams, James (Ratlidge)
Williams, Ward
Willson, ... (widow)
Willson, Allen
Willson, Ebenez[e]r
Willson, George L[an]d
Willson, Hosea
Willson, Joseph
Willson, Nathan
Willson, Rob[er]t, Jr.
Willson, Simon W.
Willson, Skidmore
Willson, Solomon
Willson, William
Willson, William (of R.)
Wiltbank, John
Woldon, John
Wood, John
Woodley, Gove
Woodley, Jon[atha]n
Wright, Ambrose
Wyatt, Thomas
Wyatt, William
Wykoff, Peter
Wynford, John
Wynford, William

Young, Nathan
Young, Noah

Free Negroes

Dublin Caldwell
Jeffrey George
Prince Bower
Absalom Gibbs
Bania
Matthew Nock
William Jinkins
Aaron Shippy
George Mifflin
Daniel Nock
Sipples Absalom
Jeffrey Bewly
Downham's Jim
John Gibbs

Virdins Toney
Virdin's Tom
Craiges Glascow
Loockermans Dave
Sipples Peter
Purdens Solomon
Furbees Jack
Lockwoods Adam
Mollistons Anthony
Jacob Grimnaye
Sipples Isaac
Gabriel Sneed
Pattens Jack
Snowhill Jim
Jim Gibbs Miller

SUSSEX COUNTY
Angola and Indian River Hundreds

Allin, W[illia]m, Land
Anderson, John
Atkins, Elijah
Atkins, Spencer
Atkins, W[illia]m
Bagwell, John
Bagwell, W[illiam], Estate
Bales, Jeams F.
Bannum, Grear
Bannum, Isaac
Barker, Bagwell
Barker, Eli
Barker, Job
Bartle, Tho[ma]s
Benston, Benja[min], Jr.
Blezzard, Stephen
Blezzard, Tho[ma]s
Blezzard, W[illia]m
Blezzard, W[illia]m, Land
Brady, John
Brerton, Hennery
Brerton, Tho[ma]s
Burbig, John
Burbig, Tho[ma]s
Burton, Aaron
Burton, Benja[min] of B.
Burton, Benja[min], saller [sailor]
Burton, Betty, Ango[la]
Burton, Daniel
Burton, Isaac
Burton, Isaiah
Burton, Jacob
Burton, James, son of Luke
Burton, Jesse
Burton, John, Ango[la]
Burton, John, Jr.

Burton, John, Sr.
Burton, Joseph, cord[wainer]
Burton, Joseph, Estate
Burton, Joseph, mill[er]
Burton, Joshua
Burton, Luke
Burton, Peter
Burton, Robert, mar[chant sic]
Burton, Strattan
Burton, W[illia]m
Burton, W[illia]m, Capt[ain]
Burton, W[illia]m, ferry
Burton, W[illia]m, Jr.
Burton, W[illia]m of R.
Burton, W[illia]m of W[illia]m
Butcher, Robert
Butcher, W[illia]m, car[penter]
Butcher, W[illia]m, Sr.
Cary, Eli
Cary, Joseph
Cary, Samuel
Clark, W[illia]m of David
Clark, W[illia]m, Sr.
Coffin, Nehemiah
Collins, Horatia
Collins, John
Collins, John, Jr.
Collins, Tho[ma]s
Cornish, Samuel
Cornwall, James
Corse, John
Corse, W[illia]m
Crage, David
Crage, John, Estate
Crage, Robert, Estate
Davidson, Clapool

Davidson, Jeames
Davidson, John
Davidson, Richard
Davidson, W[illia]m
Deen, Callob [Caleb]
Deen, Jesse
Derrexson, James

Ennis, W[illia]m
Ennis, W[illia]m B., Estate

Feild, John
Fisher, Samuel, Land
Foset, W[illia]m
Frame, George
Frame, John
Frame, Smith, Land

Game, John
Goodwine, Mikel
Goslee, John
Green, Gorge
Grice, Tho[ma]s
Grice, W[illia]m, Estate

Hall, Ed[war]d
Hancock, Callob [Caleb]
Handcock, John
Handcock, Micajah
Hanzer, Aaron
Hanzer, Aminidal
Hanzer, Jehu
Hanzer, John
Hanzer, Jonathan, Jr.
Hanzer, Samuel
Hanzer, Tho[ma]s
Hanzer, W[illia]m of D.
Hanzer, W[illia]m H.
Harges, Jacob
Harras, W[illia]m
Harris, Tho[ma]s
Hathaway, Wolsey, Land
Hazzard, David
Hemmons, John, Estate
Hemmons, Tho[ma]s
Hill, Gorge
Hill, Levi
Hill, Nehemiah
Hoge, Gameg E.
Hopkins, David
Hopkins, John, Land
Hopkins, John
Hopkins, Joseph
Hopkins, Samuel
Hopkins, W[illia]m
Houston, Joseph
Houston, Micajah, Land
Hudson, Walter

Jackson, Annias

Jackson, Francis
Jackson, James
Johnson, Edw[ard]
Johnson, Milby
Johnson, Samuel
Johnson, W[illia]m, Jr.
Johnson, W[illia]m, Sr.
Jones, Mary
Jones, W[illia]m
Joseph, Hezekiah
Joseph, Isaac
Joseph, Jerimiah
Joseph, Jonathan
Joseph, Joseph
Joseph, Nathan
Joseph, Purnel
Joseph, Zackriah
Joster, Tho[ma]s

King, Ephram

Lacey, Hezkiah
Lacey, Robert
Lacey, Spencer
Lacey, W[illia]m
Lawson, James
Lewes, Noble
Lingo, Henry
Lingo, John
Lingo, Peter
Lingo, Samuel

McDowell, Elias
McDowell, Isaac
McDowell, Moses
McIlvain, Abel
McIlvain, Andrew, **Estate**
McIlvain, Benja[min]
McIlvain, Comfort
McIlvain, David
McIlvain, Lenard

Marriner, Constant
Marriner, Gorge, Land
Marriner, Moses
Marriner, Robert
Marriner, Tho[ma]s, Land
Martin, Joseph
Martin, W[illia]m
Massey, W[illia]m
Meegee, John
Melby, Nanney
Milby, Levin, Land
Milby, Nath[anie]l, Land
Morgen, W[illia]m
Morris, John, smith
Morris, Joshua, mill

Norwood, Eli

Oaky, W[illia]m

Olever, James
Owens, Worrinton

Parker, Anderson, Estate
Parsons, Robert
Pool, John, Jr.
Pool, John, Sr.
Pool, Mager
Pool, Perry
Pool, W[illia]m
Prettyman, Burton, Estate
Prettyman, Joseph
Prettyman, Robert of W[illia]m
Prettyman, W[illia]m, (R.)
Prid, James
Prid, James, Jr.
Prittyman, Benja[min]
Prittyman, Robert, (R.)
Prittyman, Robert, Estate
Prittyman, Tho[ma]s
Prittyman, W[illia]m
Prittyman, W[illia]m, (R.)
Prittyman, W[illia]m D.

Reckcords, Tho[ma]s
Reed, Allin, Estate
Reed, Nehemiah, Jr.
Reed, Nehemiah, Sr.
Regwar, Isaac
Regwar, John
Richards, Benja[min]
Richards, David
Richards, Jacob
Rider, Betty
Rider, John
Rigwar, W[illia]m
Roach, James
Roach, Levi
Robenson, Joseph
Robinson, Benj[amin]
Robinson, Peter
Robinson, Tho[ma]s, Estate
Robinson, W[illia]m
Rust, David
Rust, John, Land
Rust, Jonathan
Rust, Peter

Salmans, John
Salmons, Isaac R.
Sempler, Andrew, Jr.
Sempler, Tho[ma]s
Sempler, W[illia]m, Jr.
Sharp, James, Estate
Shockley, Solomon, Estate
Shockley, Jacob, Estate
Shankland, W[illia]m

Shurman, James
Shurman, John, Estate
Shurman, Tho[ma]s, Jr.
Shurman, Tho[ma]s, Sr.
Simpler, W[illia]m, Jr.
Smith, Marshel
Spear, John
Stephenson, Hugh
Stephenson, James
Stephenson, Jonathan
Stephenson, Robert, Estate
Stephenson, W[illia]m, son of Jona[than]
Stockley, Betty
Stockley, John, carp[enter]
Stockley, John, Sr.
Stockley, Woodman, Jr.
Stockley, Woodman, Sr.
Stockly, Cornel[iu]s, Estate
Street, Jeremiah
Surman, Tho[ma]s, Sr.

Thompson, Adam
Thompson, Andrew
Toomy, John
Toomy, Nehemiah
Toomy, Tho[ma]s
Townsend, Jesse, Land

Vaughn, Charles
Vaughn, Joseph
Vaughn, W[illia]m

Wall, James
Waller, Nelson
Walls, Joshua, Jr.
Walls, Levin
Walls, W[illia]m, Jr.
Walls, W[illia]m, Sr.
Waples, Benja[min]
Waples, Burton, Estate
Waples, Burton, Esq.
Waples, Nathanel, Esq.
Waples, Peter
Waples, Samuel, Land
Waples, Stockley, Estate
Waples, Tho[ma]s, Sr.
Wapls, Joseph
Wapls, Tho[ma]s, Jr.
Warrinton, Luke
West, Benjamin, Estate
West, Elias, Estate
West, Ezekiel, Estate
White, Jacob
White, Nucomb
Whorton, Charls
Wilkins, James
Williams, Jesse
Williams, John, Land

Willson, Tho[ma]s
Wilson, James
Wilson, Joshua
Woolf, W[illia]m
Worrenton, Levi
Worrinton, Benja[min]

Worrinton, Joseph
Worrinton, Robert
Worrinton, Tho[ma]s
Worrinton, W[illia]m
Wright, Gorge
Wyatt, Jehu
Wyatt, Joseph

Baltimore Hundred

Ake, Riley
Ake, William
Aydelott, Benjamin
Aydelott, Cornelias
Aydelott, David
Aydelott, John, B. L.
Aydelott, John [of] [Sam[ue]l
Aydelott, John, Sr.
Aydelott, Samuel

Bacor, John
Banks, Jacob
Barker, Richard
Barker, Zadock
Barns, Elizabeth
Bassett, Richard, L[an]d
Batson, Thomas, Esq.
Bishop, Edward
Black, Samuel
Brasure, William
Bridell, Elihu
Brintin, Jonathan
Buckworth, John

Campbell, John
Campbell, John, Sr.
Capbell, William
Clark, Levin
Coffien, Thomas
Coffin, Comfort
Collins, Noah
Cord, Shibna
Cropper, James
Cropper, Thomas
Cropper, William

Dazey, John
Dazey, Jonathan
Dazey, Joseph
Dazey, Moses
Dazey, Thomas
Dazey, Thomas, Jr.
Dennis, John, L[an]d
Dirickson, Andrcase
Dirickson, George
Dirickson, Handy
Dirickson, Isaiah
Dirickson, Job
Dirickson, Samuel

Ellis, William

Esham, Jacob
Evans, Catherein
Evans, Daniel
Evans, Ebenezer
Evans, Eli
Evans, Elijah
Evans, Elisha
Evans, Enoch
Evans, Hannah
Evans, Isaac
Evans, Jacob
Evans, Jacob
Evans, John, Const[able]
Evans, John of Eby
Evans, John, Sr.
Evans, Samuel
Evans, Solomon
Evans, Solomon, Sr.
Evans, Thomas, cord[wainer]
Evans, William
Evans, William R.

Fossit, James, L[an]d
Fossits, Elijah, L[an]d
Fossitt, Smith, L[an]d
Freeman, Jedadiah
Freeman, Job
Freeman, Zachariah
Freeman, Zephaniah

Gibbins, Jonathan
Godwine, Rhoda
Gray, Howard
Gray, Isaac
Gray, Jeams
Gray, Jesse, L[an]d
Gray, Thomas
Gray, William

Hall, William
Hall, William J., Esq.
Hambling, John, L[an]d
Handcock, Frederick
Harney, Thomas, Jr.
Hatfield, John
Hazzard, John
Hickman, Richard
Hickman, Selby
Hill, Brithtunham
Hill, Elizabeth

Hill, John S.
Hill, Levin
Holland, Benjamin
Holland, Elizabeth
Holland, Elizabeth of W.
Howard, George
Howard, Nehemiah
Hudson, Ananias
Hudson, David
Hudson, Jaquish
Hudson, John
Hudson, John of Jaq.
Hudson, Mary
Hudson, Miles, heirs
Hudson, Richard
Hudson, Scofield
Hudson, Thomas, L[an]d

Irons, Aaron
Irons, David
Irons, Lemuel
Irons, Rachel

Jacobs, John
Johnson, Henry
Johnson, Isaac
Johnson, Rachel
Johnson, William
Johnson, John
Johnson, Job
Johnson, Luke
Johnson, Peter
Jones, Dagworthy
Jones, Jesse, L[an]d
Jones, John, Esq.

Knox, Solomon

Larrance, Henry
Laughinghouse, William
Leggit, John
Lockwood, William
Long, Benjamin

McCabe, Arthur
McCabe, John, Jr.
McCabe, John, Sr.
McCabe, Obediah
Madox, Mary
Massey, Isaiah
Massey, John, Jr.
Massey, John, Sr.
Mifflin, Daniel, L[and]d
Miller, Bershaba
Miller, James
Murrah, David
Murrah, James
Murrah, James, H. S.

Nicholson, Samuel, heirs

Powders, Revel
Powders, William

Powel, Walter
Powel, William
Powel, Zadock, L[an]d
Purnal, Walter, heirs, L[an]d
Purnals, Thomas, L[an]d

Quinton, James, L[an]d

Rickards, Eli
Rickards, Elias
Rickards, Elisha
Rickards, John
Rickards, Mary
Rickards, William, H. S.
Rickards, William, Sr.
Roberts, Mary
Roberts, Sanders
Roberts, William
Rogers, Agness
Rogers, Isaac
Rogers, Jacob
Rogers, Mathew

Selby, Thomas, L[an]d
Styers, Stephen

Taylor, Andrew
Taylor, Betty
Taylor, Tandy
Taylor, Thomas
Taylor, William
Tingle, James
Tingle, Jesper
Tingle, John
Tingle, Littleton
Tingle, Luke
Tingle, Thomas
Tingle, William
Townsand, Job
Townsand, Littleton
Truitt, Andrew
Truitt, William
Tubbs, David
Tunnell, Elizabeth
Tunnell, Scarbrough
Turner, Levi
Tyer, Thomas, L[an]d

Walters, Peleg, heirs, L[an]d
Waters, Joseph, L[an]d
West, Amos
West, Caleb
West, Jacob
West, John
West, Mary
West, Ruben
West, Sarah
West, Thomas
West, William
Whaley, Charles
Wharton, Betty

Wharton, Daniel
Wharton, Francis
Wharton, Isaiah
Wharton, James
Wharton, Jonathan
Wharton, Mary
Wharton, Mathew

Wildgoose, Joseph
Wildgoose, Robert
Wildrige, Leah
Williams, Andrew, Jr.
Williams, Andrew, Sr.
Williams, Arther
Williams, Edward
Williams, Ezekiel

BROADKILL HUNDRED

Abbet, Baker
Abbet, Nicholas
Abbet, Richard, L[an]d
Abbet, William
Abbet, William
Atkins, Isaac

Baines, Robert
Baker, Elias
Baker, John
Baker, Solomon
Baley, Jonathan
Banium, William
Bannum, Henary
Banum, George
Banum, Levy
Bedford, Guning, L[an]d
Bennet, Purnal
Birton, Joshua
Bivens, Benjamin
Bivens, Leven
Bivens, Roland
Bivens, Thomas
Black, Elizabeth
Bloxsom, Moses
Bloxsom, William
Bloxum, Richard, Estate
Bloxum, Unice
Bloxura, Richard, Jr.
Brumble, Major
Burton, Mary
Butler, Benjamin
Butler, John
Butler, Samuel

Cade, John, Estate
Cade, John, Junior
Cade, Richerson
Cade, Richerson, Jr.
Cammel, John
Campel, Ester
Carey, Thomas
Carey, William
Carpenter, Jacob
Carpenter, Samuel
Carpenter, William
Cary, John, Sr.
Chace, James

Clapole, George
Clark, John
Clark, Miers
Clifton, Aaron, L[an]d
Clifton, Phillip
Clow, John, Esq., Estate
Colhoon, Jonathan
Collings, Darby
Collins, Eli
Collins, John, Estate
Collins, Thomas
Colter, Andrew
Colter, Eli
Colter, James, cordwainer
Colter, John
Colter, Robert
Conally, Charles
Conway, Williams, L[an]d
Conwell, Abraham
Conwell, Avery
Conwell, Craudis
Conwell, David
Conwell, Elias
Conwell, Frances
Conwell, George
Conwell, George
Conwell, John, Jr.
Conwell, John, Sr.
Conwell, Shephard
Conwell, William
Cord, Mary
Cord, William
Cordary, James
Costen, Joshua
Costen, Mathias
Costen, Somuset
Costen, Stephen
Coulter, James
Coulter, John, L[an]d
Coulter, Joseph
Coulter, Thomas
Coulter, William
Coverdall, Isaac
Coverdall, Richard
Coverdall, Samuel
Coverdall, William

Daugherty, James
Daughters, Hossey
Davis, Richard
Davis, Zorababel
Day, John
Delaney, William
Deputy, Nunes
Dickerson, Edmond
Dickerson, Edmond, Jr.
Dickerson, Jonathan
Dickerson, Jonathan
Dickerson, Jonathan, Jr.
Dickerson, Leven
Dickerson, William
Dickerson, William, Sr.
Dingee, Daniel, L[an]d
Dirrum, George
Donafin, James
Donafin, Woolman
Donafun, Foster
Donavan, Azriah, Jr.
Donofan, John
Donofun, Foster, Sr.
Donovan, Abraham
Donovan, Woolman, L[an]d
Dood, Aaron
Dood, Emanuel
Dood, George
Dood, Joseph
Dood, Nathan
Dood, Pillijah
Dood, Samuel
Dood, Solomon, Jr.
Dood, Solomon, Sr.
Dorman, John S.
Douney, Jonathan
Draper, Isaac
Dukes, Jesse
Duten, James
Dutton, Abel
Dutton, Baker
Dutton, Isaac
Dutton, Jesse
Dutton, John
Dutton, Thomas

Eldate, James
Ennas, John
Evans, Thomas

Finwicks, William
Firman, David
Fisher, James, L[an]d
Fisher, John
Fist, Simeon
Fitchell, William
Fleetwood, John
Fleetwood, Joseph

Flemming, Archabeld
Fosset, Eli
Fowlar, William, (of John)
Fowler, John
Fowler, William, (of W[illia]m)
Frame, Robert
Frame, William
Fugus, James

Glover, Joshua
Gorden, George
Gray, Frazer
Green, Ezekel, Jr.
Green, Samuel
Gren, Ezekel
Gum, Abram, L[an]d
Gum, Abram, Jr., L[an]d
Gum, Hanah, L[an]d
Gum, John, L[an]d
Gum, Roger, L[an]d
Gum, William C.

Hairis, Abraham
Hall, Azail
Hall, Casa
Hall, James (son of Jos[eph])
Hall, John
Hall, John (son of Th[omas])
Hall, Joseph
Hall, Joseph (son of Jon[athan])
Hall, Joshua
Hall, Levy
Hall, Robert
Hall, William (son of Jos[eph])
Hall, William, tailor
Hand, John, (of Jos[eph])
Hand, William
Haris, Aberaham
Harmon, Azgel
Harris, Benton
Hart, Richard
Hart, Thomas
Hart, Zachariah
Haveloe, Daniel, L[an]d
Haverloe, John
Haverlow, Anthoney
Haverlow, Hanah
Haverlow, James
Hazard, Annah
Hazard, Joseph, Esq.
Hazard, William
Hazle, John
Hazzard, Card [Cord]
Hazzard, Hap
Hazzard, Jacob
Hazzard, John
Henmon, Ezekel
Heverlow, Andrew

Hickman, Nathaniel
Hobson, John
Holand, John
Holston, William
Hood, Robert
Hopkins, Archabold
Hoverllow, Roderick
Hoverlow, Antoney, Jr.
Hoverlow, Jonathan
Hudson, Anderson
Hudson, Robert (Decd.)
Hudson, Samuel, Estate
Ingram, John
Jackson, Clemint
James, Zadoc
Janson, James
Jeffers, Nathen
Jeffers, William
Jefferson, Warren
Jester, Daniel
Jones, Abigail
Jones, Abigal
Jones, Elias
Jones, Elizabeth
Jones, Griffith
Jones, John
Jones, Robert
Jones, Samuel (son of Ct.)
Jonson, Benjamin
Jonson, Birton
Joseph, Elisha
Kimey, Aron
King, David
King. James
King, John, L[an]d
King, William
Lank, James
Lank, John
Lank, Leven
Lank, Mitchel
Lank, Thomas
Lay, Baptis
Lecats, Jobe
Lecatt, Leven
Lecatt, Michel
Lewes, Adam
Lindell, Zadac
Lofland, Gaberiel
Lott, Charles
Luker, William
McCormick, Thomas
McKnight, James
Mackling, Job
Manlove, Roberson, L[an]d
Manloves, David

Marter, John
Martin, John
Marvel, Thomas
Mason, Joseph
Matthews, William, L[an]d
Mechafee, Daniel
Messah, George
Messakes, Isaac
Messakes, Job
Messakes, John
Messakes, Obediah
Michel, Stephen
Mifland, Sarah
Milis, David
Miller, Augustus
Miller, William
Missah, Levy, Estate
Missakes, Patience
Mitten, Isaac
Mitten, William, Sr.
Morgan, John
Morgan, Joshua, Jr.
Morgan, Parker
Morgin, Richard
Morress, Joseph (Little)
Morriss, Bivens
Morriss, Dennes, Jr.
Morriss, Dennis, Sr.
Morriss, Joseph
Morriss, Joshua
Morriss, William
Mumford, Frances, L[an]d
Neell, Robert
Notingham, Abel
Notingham, Jacob
Nucoumb, Thomas
Oens, William
Okey, Elizabeth, L[an]d
Palmore, Job
Palmore, John
Palmore, Mary
Palmore, Richard
Palmore, William, (of K.)
Parmor, Curtis
Parmor, William, L[an]d
Parmore, Stephen
Patterson, Hugh
Patterson, Hugh
Pepper, Eli
Pepper, John
Pepper, Leven
Pettyjohn, Ebenezer
Pettyjohn, John
Pilijahn, Zachariah
Pinter, Samuel
Pipper, Joshua

Pittyjohn, Aaron
Pittyjohn, James
Ponder, James
Pride, Job
Pride, John, L[an]d
Pride, Thomas
Pullet, Levin
Pury, Aaron
Pury, William, Esq.
Records, Benjamin
Records, James
Reding, Stephen
Reed, Absalum
Reed, Edmon
Reed, James
Reed, Job, Jr.
Reed, Job, Sr.
Reed, John, Constable
Reed, Joshua
Reed, Matthew
Reed, Nathan
Reed, Zachariah
Reley, William
Reynals, Richard
Reynals, Thomas
Reynals, Thomas
Reynals, Zachariah
Riley, John
Riliy, Jacob
Riliy, Lawrence
Roach, Daniel
Robins, Charles
Robins, Levy, Estate
Robins, William
Roch, John
Rodgers, Lasurs
Roland, James
Roland, John
Roland, John, Estate
Roland, Samuel, L[and]d
Ross, Edmon
Rouse, John
Rusel, Emanuel
Russel, Levy
Russell, Samuel
Ruth, Christopher
Samons, Eli
Samons, Joseph
Savag, Roberson, L[an]d
Scidmore, Elizabeth
Seudder, David, L[an]d
Sharpe, Jacob
Sharpe, Job
Sharpe, John
Shelpmon, Cornelous
Shelpmon, William

Shockley, Rhods
Simpler, Aaron
Simpler, Andrew
Simpler, Milby
Skidmor, Henery
Smith, Coltin
Smith, Thomas Watson
Spencer, Nathen
Stafford, John
Stave, James
Steel, Benjamin
Steel, Samuel
Steel, William
Stephenson, John
Stephson, James
Stephson, John
Stewarts, Ann, L[an]d
Stewarts, Mary, L[an]d
Stuard, David
Stuart, Elizabeth
Stuart, John
Stuart, John A.
Stuart, Thomas
Talbard, John
Talbirt, Robert
Tam, John
Tam, Joseph
Thomas, Luke
Thornigton, David
Tinley, John
Tinley, Jonathan, L[an]d
Tinley, Stringe, L[an]d
Tinley, Stringer
Truett, Peter
Tull, John
Tull, William
Turner, Lazarus
Vent, John
Virden, Levy
Virden, Manlove
Virden, Marnix
Virden, William
Walker, John, L[an]d
Wallers, Charles, Estate
Walles, Samuel
Warren, Ebenezar
Warren, Eli
Warren, Jobe
Warren, Kendale
Warren, Lodywick
Warren, Mager
Warren, Richard
Warren, Samuel
Warrington, John A.
Warrington, Stephen
Warton, Rixsom
Watson, Thomas

Welch, Jacob
Welch, Jacob
West, George
West, Thomas
Wheelbank, Samuel
Wiatte, William
Wight, Samuel, L[an]d
Wiley, James
Williams, Nathanel
Willis, Robert
Willson, Isaac

Willson, James
Willson, John
Willson, Reubi
Willson, Thomas
Willson, William
Wilson, Thomas, Jr.
Wiltbank, Cornelius
Woods, Stephen
Wright, Nathaniel
Wright, Peter F.
Young, William

CEDAR CREEK HUNDRED

Abbot, George
Abbot, James
Abbot, John, L[an]d
Abbot, Nickless
Abbot, William, Jr.
Ansoley, Samuel
Arnol, John

Beachamp, Isaac
Beckworth, Soloman
Bennett, John, (minor), L[an]d
Bennett, Joshua
Bennett, Nehemiah
Bennett, Purnal, (minor), L[an]d
Bivans, Comfort, (minor), L[an]d
Bivans, John, (minor), L[an]d
Bivans, Mary, (minor), L[an]d
Bivans, Thomas, (minor), L[an]d
Black, Adam
Black, George
Bloxsom, Richard
Bourrough, William
Brown, Israel
Bryan, James
Bryan, Jonathan
Bryan, Shephard

Campbell, John S.
Carlile, Bowen
Carlile, Daniel
Carlile, Pemberton
Carlile, Thomas
Carlile, William, L[an]d
Carlile, Zaciriah
Carpenter, Nephati
Cary, Amos, L[an]d
Cary, Charles
Cary, Nehemiah
Cary, Thomas, (joiner)
Cary, Thomas, Sr.
Cears, Jonathan
Cheveleer, Peter
Clifton, Allen

Clifton, Isaac
Clifton, Jehu
Clifton, Nathan, L[an]d
Clindaniel, Ahab
Clindaniel, Avary
Clindaniel, John
Clindaniel, John, Jr.
Clindaniel, Luke, L[an]d
Cobner, Spencer
Coffen, William
Cole, Coverdill
Cole, Draper
Collings, Asa
Collings, Hancock, L[an]d
Collings, John, L[an]d
Collings, John, son of Joseph
Collings, John, Jr.
Collings, Joseph
Collings, Richard
Collings, Samuel
Collings, Warner
Collings, William
Conner, Bundick
Cooke, George
Couch, Perey
Coverdill, John
Coverdill, Richard
Coverdill, Thomas
Cowin, George
Craper, John, L[an]d
Crapper, Molton, (minor)
Crapper, Zadoc
Curwithin, Caleb

Daniel, Abram
Daniel, Thomas
Daniel, William, Jr.
Daniel, William, Sr.
Davis, Abishai
Davis, Calab
Davis, Manlove
Davis, Mark
Davis, Nehemiah

Davis, Peter
Davis, Thomas
Davis, William
Depray, Selby
Deputy, Boaz
Deputy, Charles
Deputy, Jesse
Deputy, Joshua, L[an]d
Deputy, Soloman
Deputy, Sylvester
Deputy, Vester
Deputy, William
Donophin, Edmon
Donophin, Woolman
Dows, Leven
Dows, Leven, L[an]d
Drapper, Alexander
Drapper, Avary
Drapper, Charles
Drapper, John, (minor)
Drapper, William
Dryden, William

Eldridge, Obediah
Evans, Ebenezzer
Evans, Thomas, Esq.

Fisher, John
Fisher, Joshua
Fisher, Joshua, L[an]d
Fisher, Samuel, L[an]d
Fisher, Thomas
Fisher, Thomas, L[an]d
Fleetwood, Thomas
Flemmon, Joseph
Fountain, Andrew
Fountain, Marcy

Gray, Elijah
Griffith, Joram
Guy, Mager

Hall, James
Hambleton & Till's, L[an]d
Hammon, Isaac
Hand, Thomas
Hayes, Curtes
Hayes, John
Hayes, Joshua
Hayes, Luke
Hayes, Manlove
Hayes, Nathaniel
Hayes, Purnal
Hayes, Richard, Jr.
Hayes, Richard, the 3rd
Hayes, Thomas

Hazalet, Joseph, L[an]d
Hazzard, George
Heaveloe, Ruben
Hickman, Jacob
Hickman, John
Hickman, Rachel
Hickman, William
Hill, Nathan, (minor), L[an]d
Hill, Robert
Hill, Robert, (minor), L[an]d
Hinds, William
Hodgler, Jonathan
Holedger, Nathaniel, L[an]d
Holston, Joseph
Holston, Joseph, Jr.
Holston, Robert, L[an]d
Hudson, Henery
Hudson, Job
Hudson, John, cupper
Hudson, John, Jr.
Hudson, John, Sr.
Hudson, Jonathan
Hudson, Joseph
Hudson, Joshua
Hudson, Richard
Hudson, Seth
Hudson, Solomon
Hudson, William, Sr.

Ireland, Samuel

Jester, John
Johnson, Bacon
Johnson, James
Johnson, James
Johnson, Peter
Johnson, William
Johnson, William, L[an]d

Kendrick, William
Killingworth, John
Killingworth, John, Jr.
Killingworth, William
Killo, John
Killo, Joseph

Laws, Belitha
Laws, Joshua
Layton, Alexander
Layton, Isaac
Layton, John
Lewis, Semon
Lickount, James
Linsey, Frances
Lofland, Branson
Lofland, Charles

Lofland, George
Lofland, Grace
Lofland, James
Lofland, John
Lofland, Joshua
Lofland, Littleton
Lofland, Nutter
Lofland, Rachel
Lofland, William
Lofland, Zadoc, L[an]d

Mckey, James
Mckey, William
Mclain, Charles
Marcy, Joshua
May, Drapper, Estate
May, Philops
Meloney, William
Messick, George
Metcalf, John
Millan, Robert
Milman, Peter
Moore, John
Moore, William
Morgin, Thomas
Morris, Elihu
Morris, George, L[an]d
Morris, Nimrod
Munlicks, Israel
Murphy, Isaac
Murrah, John

Nutter, John

Oliver, Aaron
Oliver, Benjamin
Oliver, Levi
Ousburn, Thomas
Ousten, Isaac
Owins, Robert
Owins, Samuel

Palmore, Alexander
Pointer, Nathaniel (B)
Pointer, Nathaniel (N. son)
Pointer, Ratlove
Pointer, Thomas
Pointer, William
Pointer, William (W[illia]m's son)
Polk, Edward
Polk, Ephraim, Jr.
Polk, Ephram
Polk, Joab
Polk, Joseph
Polk, William
Postels, John
Postels, Shadrick

Postels, Thomas
Potter, Edward
Potter, John
Potter, Sego
Preteman, Pery
Preteman, Woodman
Pride, Luke
Pride, William
Pullet, Thomas, L[an]d
Purnal, John
Purnal, Thomas, L[an]d
Ratlove, Samuel
Reed, Jesse
Reiley, George
Rench, James
Richards, John
Richards, John, Jr.
Richards, Joseph
Richards, Joseph, Jr.
Richards, Spencer
Rickards, John, L[an]d
Richards, John (Kent)
Rickards, George
Rickards, Luke
Rickards, Mills
Rickards, Staton
Rickards, Thomas
Rickards, William
Rickards, William, Jr.
Rickards, Zadoc
Riggs, Ezekiel
Riggs, Isaac
Riggs, Levi
Riley, Beniamin
Riley, William
Robenson, Burton
Robenson, Charles
Robenson, John
Robenson, John, Jr.
Rogers, Daniel
Ross, James

Sharp, Selby
Shaver, Ann
Shaver, John
Shiphard, John
Shockley, Curtes
Shockley, Eli
Shockley, James
Shockley, Leven, L[an]d
Shockley, Rhods
Shockley, William, Jr.
Shockley, William, Sr.
Shors, William
Simpson, Benjamin
Smith, Allen
Smith, Betty, (minor), L[an]d

Smith, David
Smith, David, tailor
Smith, Henery
Smith, Jesse
Smith, Job
Smith, John
Smith, John (Primhook)
Smith, Sarah, (minor), L[an]d
Smith, Thomas
Smith, William
Spencer, Donophin
Spencer, Ebenezer
Spencer, Iszaiel
Spencer, Jesse, L[an]d
Spencer, John
Spencer, Levi
Spencer, Luke
Spencer, Nathan
Spencer, Noah
Spencer, Samuel
Srowden, Aaron
Stapelford, Castilley
Stapelford, Edward
Stockley, Joseph
Stockley, Nathaniel, (minor), L[an]d
Stockley, Woodman
Sturgis, Shadrick

Till & Hambleton's, L[an]d
Townsend, Benjamin
Townsend, Elias
Townsend, Jacob
Townsend, Job
Townsend, John
Townsend, Littleton
Townsend, Luke, L[an]d
Townsend, Mager
Townsend, Polly, (minor), L[an]d
Townsend, Stephen, L[an]d
Townsend, William
Truett, Soloman, L[an]d
Truitt, Collings
Truitt, John
Truitt, Joseph
Truitt, Lankford
Truitt, Weldon
Truitt, William
Truitt, Zadoc
Turner, Leven, L[an]d
Turner, Levi

Vankurk, Barnut, L[an]d
Vankurk, David
Vankurk, George
Vankurk, John
Vankurk, William

Veach, Elias
Veach, Purnol
Veach, Solomon
Veach, Thomas, Jr.
Veach, William
Viney, Phebe, L[an]d
Vist, Andrew

Waller, Ann
Walls, Howard
Walls, William
Walton, David, L[an]d
Walton, George, Jr.
Walton, George, Sr.
Walton, John
Walton, Jonathan
Walton, Joseph
Walton, Luke, L[an]d
Walton, Watson
Walton, William
Warbrook, Andrew
Ward, William
Warren, Bennett
Wattsan, William
Wattson, Betheuel, (D. son)
Wattson, Bethuel
Wattson, Bethuel, Jr.
Wattson, Isaac, (I's son)
Wattson, Jesse
Wattson, John, L[an]d
Wattson, Joseph
Wattson, Luke
Wattson, Luke, Sr.
Wattson, Robert, Jr.
Wattson, Robert, Sr.
Wattson, William, L[an]d
Webb, Charles
Webb, Dorman
Webb, Jacob
Webb, Jacob. Jr.
Webb, John, L[an]d
Webb, Jonas
Webb, Obediah
Webb, Sylvester
Webb, Thomas
Welles, Rice
Wharton, John
Whealler, Noah
Wheallers, John, L[an]d
Williams, Curtis
Williams, David
Williams, Eli
Williams, Henery
Williams, John
Williams, Jonathan

Williams, Limuel
Williams, Morgin
Williams, William
Wills, Henery
Wilson, John
Wilson, Thomas
Wilson, William
Worren, Absalem
Worren, Alexander

Worren, Charles
Worren, Levi
Worren, Parker
Worren, Wrixsom

Young, Beniamin
Young, John
Young, Nathaniel, Esq.
Young, Robert, L[an]d

DAGSBORO HUNDRED

Aydelote, Isaac

Babins, Zachariah
Bailey, Jonathan
Beanum, Levi
Benston, Spencer
Betts, Jeams
Betts, Jonathan
Brookfield, Uriah, Estate
Burton, Jacob
Burton, Woolsey

Cary, Ebinezar
Cary, Elijah
Cary, John, (son of E.)
Cary, John, (son of W[illia]m)
Cary, Soloman
Cary, Thomas
Cassons, Joseph
Collings, Elijah
Collings, George
Collings, Isaac
Collings, John
Cottingham, Elisha
Cottingham, Joshua

Dayworthy, John, Estate
Dericson, Joseph
Derrecson, John
Dickerson, Elisha
Dingle, Edward, Esq.
Dingle, William

Evans, Walter
Evins, John, tailor
Evins, William
Evins, William

Freeman, Michael
Freeman, William

Gautt, Thomas
Goslee, Job
Goslee, William, Estate
Gray, Isaac

Hall, Peter
Hall, William
Hardy, Joshua
Harmon, Edward
Harmon, Gorge
Harper, Thomas
Hazzard, Thomas
Hichens, Isaac
Hichens, William
Hopkins, Gorge
Hopkins, Robert
Hopkins, Robirt, smith
Houston, Joseph
Houston, Robert
Howel, John
Howel, William

Ingram, Collings
Ingram, Jacob
Ingram, Job
Ingram, Joshua
Ingram, Robert, Estate
Ingram, Robert, Jr.
Ingram, Thomas

Jacobs, Abraham
Jefferson, Elihu
Jefferson, Job
Jefferson, John
Jefferson, Joshua
Jefferson, Richard
Johnson, Bartholomew
Johnson, Benjamin
Johnson, Dannal
Johnson, Isaiah
Johnson, John
Jones, James
Jones, Miles
Jones, Thomas, Jr.
Jones, Thomas, Sr.
Jones, Wingat
Jones, Zakariah

Killum, Jesse
Killum, Thomas

Killum, William
Kimmy, Sanders
Kollock, Simon

Lockwood, Armwell
Lockwood, Benjemen
Lockwood, Benjemen
Lockwood, Samuel
Long, Armwell
Long, David
Long, David, Sr.

Marvil, Aron
Marvil, David
Marvil, Parker
Marvil, Phillip
Marvil, Prittyman
Marvil, Robert
Marvil, Stephen
Marvil, Thomas
Marvil, Thomas
Marvil, William
Massey, William
Meeres, Ezekile
Meers, Robert
Messeck, Coventon
Messeek, Eli
Messeek, George
Messeek, Isaac
Messeek, Isaac
Messeek, Mines
Mitchel, William C.
Mitchell, George
Moore, David
Moore, James
Moore, John
Moore, William, Jr.
Moore, William, Sr.
Morris, Burton
Morris, Isaac
Morris, John
Morris, Lacey
Morris, Robert
Morris, William
Morriss, Bibins, Estate
Morriss, Isaac
Morriss, Jacob
Morriss, John
Morriss, Joseph
Morriss, Joshua
Mumfort, John

Newbold, William
Newton, William

Otwell, Frances
Otwell, William
Otwell, William, Sr.

Parsons, Robert
Petted, Edward
Phillips, Benjamin
Phillips, Benjamin, Jr.
Phillips, John
Phillips, John, Jr.
Pinter, Thomas
Piper, Joseph
Piper, William
Powell, Levi
Prittyman, Burton
Prittyman, George
Prittyman, Robert
Prittyman, Thomas
Prittyman, Thomas, L[an]d
Prittyman, Thomas, (son of Rob[er]t)
Prittyman, William
Prittyman, Zachariah

Ragla, William
Roach, Samual
Robinson, Joseph
Robinson, Joshua
Robinson, Joshua, smith
Rodney, William, Jr.
Rodny, Thomas
Rodny, William
Rogers, George
Rogers, John
Rolings, Charles
Russle, William

Sammons, William
Samons, Benjeamen
Samons, James
Samons, Soloman
Schofield, William
Scot, Michel
Sharp, William, Estate
Short, Craffort
Short, Edward, Jr.
Short, Edward, Sr.
Short, Isaac, Sr.
Short, Jacob
Short, Job
Short, John
Short, Phillip, Estate
Short, Samuel
Sockam, James
Steen, James

Teague, William
Tindal, . . ., Widdow
Tindal, Samuel
Tingle, John
Tingle, William
Tingle, William, Jr.
Thompson, Charles
Thompson, James
Thompson, Truet
Thompson, William
Thompson, William, Sr.
Thoroughgood, . . ., Widow
Throughgood, John
Throughgood, Millar
Trueit, John
Tunel, Isaac
Tunel, Jed

Veazey, Zadock

Waplas, Eli
Waplas, Elihu
Waplas, Isaac
Waplas, Mary
Waplas, Paul
Waplas, Peter

Waplas, Thomas
Waplas, William
Watson, John
Watson, Peter
Watson, Smithers
Watson, William
West, Cary
West, Jehu
West, Robert
West, Thomas
West, Thomas, Jr.
West, Wingat
White, William
Whorton, Burton
Whorton, Henery
Whorton, Henmon
Whorton, Wrixham, Estate
Wilkens, William
Willy, Soloman
Wingat, Henery
Wingate, John, Estate
Workman, John
Workman, William
Wright, William

LITTLE CREEK HUNDRED

Anderson, John G.
Anderson, Philip

Bacon, John
Bacon, Leven, L[an]d
Badley, Decan, Land
Badley, Gedden
Badley, Samuel
Badley, Thomas
Bailey, Davis
Bailey, George
Bailey, John
Bailey, Lowder
Bailey, Samuel
Bailey, Stephen
Bailey, Thomas
Balding, Caleb
Beach, James
Beach, Jonathan
Beach, Thomas
Bennet, Edward
Bennet, George
Bennet, John
Bennet, Joshua
Bennet, William
Benston, Isaac
Benston, James
Benston, Levy
Bivvens, James

Bivvens, Shadrach
Boadley, John
Booth, John
Brown, W[illia]m
Buck, James
Bull, Manean, Lot

Callaway, Aaron
Callaway, Angelo
Callaway, Ann
Callaway, Clement
Callaway, Ebenezer, (B's son)
Callaway, Elic
Callaway, Jehue
Callaway, Jesse
Callaway, Lecar, (widow)
Callaway, Leven
Callaway, Mary
Callaway, Mathew
Callaway, Moses
Callaway, Nehemiah
Callaway, William
Cannon, James
Carter, Jonathan
Carter, Robert
Carter, Shadrach
Cathiel, Jonathan
Colhoon, Samuel
Collins, Benjamin

Collins, Isaac
Collins, John, Jr.
Collins, John, Sr.
Collins, Joseph
Collins, Joshua
Collins, Josiah
Cooper, Isaac
Cordry, John
Cormean, James
Cormean, Nathen
Cormean, Lowder
Coventon, Spenser
Coulter, William
Coulter, William
Creigh, Edward
Crouch, John
Culver, Aaron
Culver, Isaac
Culver, Moses
Culver, W[illia]m

Dashiell, James
Dashiell, John
Denason, James
Deskey, W[illia]m
Dicks, W[illia]m

Edger, Henry
Elliot, Samuel
Elliott, Daniel
Elliott, Jacob
Elliott, John
Elliott, Melson
Ellis, Benja[min]
Ellis, Stephen
Elzey, John, Jr.
Elzey, [Willia]m
Emberson, John, Jr.
Emberson, John, Sr.
Emberson, W[illia]m
English, James
English, Leven
English, Thomas
Ewart, Robert

Farling, W[illia]m M.
Figs, Gillis
Figs, Henry
Figs, Thomas
Fletcher, James
Forman, Joseph, L[an]d
Freney, Elijah
Freney, John, Jr.
Freney, John, Sr.
Freney, Thomas

Game, Betty
Game, Leven
Giles, W[illia]m
Givvens, Sarah
Goddard, Francis
Goddard, George
Goddard, Griffin
Goddard, John
Gordy, Aaron
Gordy, Jackson
Gordy, Jacob
Gordy, John
Gordy, Joshua
Goslen, George
Gravener, Lowder
Grumble, John

Haines, Horatia
Hall, Elijah
Hall, Isaac
Hall, John
Hall, Samuel
Hall, Shadrach
Hall, Winget
Handerson, Abraham
Hardy, Phillis
Harmon, Henry
Hasty, Aaron
Hasty, Archable
Hasty, Elijah
Hasty, Henry
Hasty, John
Hasty, Joshua
Hasty, Obadiah
Hasty, Solomon
Hasty, Robert
Hasty, W[illia]m, (son [of] Jos.)
Hearn, Jonathan
Hearn, Jonathan, (son of Jona.)
Hearn, Jonathan, (son of S[amuel])
Hearn, Samuel
Hearn, Samuel, (son of Ben.)
Hearn, W[illia]m
Henry, George
Hitch, Curtis
Hitch, Elijah
Hitch, Isaac
Hitch, Leven
Hodskin, Debrex
Hodskin, Isaac
Hodskin, Stephen
Hoile, John
Holder, John
Holloday, James
Holt, W[illia]m

Horsey, Isaac, L[and]
Horsey, Nathaniel
Horsey, Stephen
Hosey, Arther, Land
Hosey, John
Hosey, John, Jr.
Howard, David
Howard, George
Howard, James
Howard, W[illia]m

Iles, Samuel

James, John
James, Joshua
Johannot, George S.
Jones, Edward, Land
Jones, Elizabeth, (widow)
Jones, James
Jones, John
Jones, Thomas

Kennerly, John
Kennerly, Joshua
Kermean, James
Kersey, Benjamin
Kersey, Solomon
Kershaw, Mitchel
King, James, (son of Sothy)
King, John
King, Levy
Kinnakin, Daniel, Sr.
Kinnakin, Danil, Jr.
Kinnakin, Mathew
Kinnakin, Waitman
Kinney, Elijah
Kinney, Joshua, Land
Kirkpatrick, Hugh
Kirkpatrick, Samuel
Knowles, Charles, Land
Knowles, Ephraim
Knowles, James
Knowles, Richard, Jr.
Knowles, Richard, Sr.
Knowles, Thomas
Knowles, W[illia]m

Lankson, W[illia]m
Lecat, Milkey
Lecat, Nehemiah
Lecat, Shadrach
Lee, . . ., Docter
Linch, Isaac
Linch, John
Linch, Mickel
Lingoe, Smith
Lowe, James
Lowe, Relph, Jr.

Lowe, Relph, Sr.
Lowe, William

McBrides, W[illia]m, L[an]d
McDowel, John
McDowel, Joshua
McKever, John
Mackenzey, Alexander
Maddux, Zephiniah
Marain, Charles
Marain, Jacob
Martain, Athanathus
Marvel, Obadiah
Mastain, Jethro
Megee, Peter
Melson, Daniel
Melvin, Mashack
Melven, Thomas
Mifling, George
Mifling, George
Mitchel, Samuel
Moor, Elijah, Land
Moore, George
Moore, Horatia
Moore, John, (son [of] Isaac)
Moore, John, (son of John)
Moore, Jonathan
Moore, Nubold, Land
Moore, Robert, Land
Moore, Shiles
Moore, Solomon
Moore, Thomas, (son [of] Jes.)
Moore, Thomas, (son of Nuble)
Moore, Thomas, (B. Warter)
Moore, Thomas, (son [of] Thos.)
Moore, W[illia]m, (son of Thos.)
Morres, Hezekiah
Morris, Nehemiah
Morris, Obadiah

Nellems, John, Land
Nicklson, Hoffington

Owney, Melby
Owns, Aaron
Owns, Isaac, (son of Aaron)
Owns, John

Partrick, John
Phillips, Elijah
Phillips, Isaac
Phillips, Jacob
Phillips, Joshua
Phillips, Richard
Phillips, Richard, (son [of] D.)
Phillips, W[illia]m
Pitts, Benjamin
Polk, John, Docter

Polk, W[illia]m, Land
Prichard, John

Ready, Benjamin
Records, Eleander
Relph, George
Riggen, Major
Riggen, W[illia]m
Rimmer, John
Rimmer, Joshua
Roads, W[illia]m
Robbens, John
Robbinson, George
Rose, John
Rose, W[illia]m
Ryon, Lowder

Salmons, Ephraim
Shores, Planner
Sillaven, John
Sirman, Betty
Sirman, Jobe
Skilley, W[illia]m
Smith, Marshell
Stanford, Samuel

Tounsand, Barkely
Tresham, James
Turpen, Denward, L[an]d
Turpen, Joseph, L[an]d
Twiford, James

Vance, George
Vance, James
Vaughan, Jonathan
Vaughan, Mary
Vinson, Daniel
Vinson, George
Vinson, Isaac
Vinson, Isaac, (son [of] Nub[el]d)
Vinson, Nubeld
Waile, George, Land

Wailes, Benjamin, Land
Walker, Charles
Walker, Emanuel
Walker, John
Walker, Spenser
Waller, Ephraim
Waller, George
Waller, James, (son [of] Capt.)
Waller, James, (son [of] W[illia]m)
Waller, Jonathan
Waller, Nubold
Waller, Thomas, (of Capt.)
Waller, W[illia]m
Warde, James
Warde, Joseph
Warde, Stephen
Whaley, Ebenezar
Whaley, Isaac
Whaley, W[illia]m
Wiley, Jarret
Willey, Charles
Williams, David
Williams, Edward
Williams, John
Williams, Samuel
Williams, Samuel, (son [of] John)
Wills, Isriel
Wilson, Henry
Winsor, James
Winwright, Cannon
Wooden, Dolbey
Wooden, Elijah
Wooden, Isaac
Wooden, Peter, (son [of] Ben.)
Worren, Benjamin
Wright, Charles
Wright, Ezekiel
Wright, Ezekiel, (son [of] Chas.)
Wright, Jesse
Wright, Leven
Wright, W[illia]m, son [of] Bloys
Wright, W[illia]m, (son of Ez.)

BROAD CREEK HUNDRED

Adams, John W.
Anderson, John
Anderson, Leven
Askridge, John
Askridge, Richard
Askridge, Samuel
Askridge, W[illia]m

Bacon, Davis
Bacon, George
Baker, Handy
Baker, James

Baker, Purnal
Beacham, Charles
Beacham, Decsson
Beacham, Edmond
Bell, Nath[anie]l, merchant
Bell, William
Benson, John, preacher
Benson, John, to[i]lor
Benson, Robert
Benson, William, Jr.
Benson, William W.

Betts, John
Betts, Jonathan
Betts, Samuel, Jr.
Betts, Samuel, Sr.
Blockum, Sothe
Bounds, John (minor)
Bounds, Joseph, Estate
Boyce, Jonathan
Boyce, Robert
Boyce, William, Jr.
Boyce, William, Sr.
Brattan, Anthoney
Brattan, James
Bressingham, Peter (Negro)
Bryan, Curnelus
Bryan, William

Callaway, Isaac, Sr.
Callaway, Jesse
Callaway, Peter (son of John)
Callaway, Thomas
Cannon, Ebenezor
Cannon, Elijah
Cannon, Jacub
Cannon, Joseph, Sr.
Cannon, Winget, Esq.
Carter, Samuel
Chipman, James
Chipman, John
Clifton, Curtis
Cockayne, Thomas
Collins, Isaac
Collins, Jenney
Collins, Joseph (minor)
Collins, Lamberson
Collins, Peggey
Collins, Polley
Collins, William, Sr.
Connaway, Curtis
Connaway, Levan
Connaway, William
Conner, Thomas
Cordif, Christefor, Land
Creighton, John, L[an]d
Dognor, John
Dolby, Jonathan, Estate
Dolby, Peter, Estate
Dolby, Peter (minor)
Downey, Summerset
Downs, Jacub, Jr.
Downs, James
Downs, John

Edger, Henry, farmer
Ellegood, Robert

Ellegood, Thomas
Ellegood, William, Jr.
Ellegood, William, Sr.
Ellingsworth, Brothers
Ellingsworth, Zachariah

Forman, Joseph, Land
Franklin, Walter, Land

German, George
German, Henry
German, William, Jr.
German, William, Sr.
Gibbens, Joshua
Gordy, Benjamin
Gordy, Eli
Gordy, John
Grace, John, Jr.
Grace, John, Sr.
Grifeth, John
Grifeth, Oliver
Gulley, James
Gunby, Betty
Gunby, James
Gunby, Stephen

Hearn, Clemmant
Hearn, Daniel
Hearn, Ebenezor, Estate
Hearn, Nehemiah
Hitchens, Charles
Hitchens, Edmond, Jr.
Hitchens, Edmond, Sr.
Hitchens, Elihu
Hitchens, Jarod, Jr.
Hitchens, John
Hitchens, Leven S., Estate
Hitchens, Mark
Hobbs, William
Hood, James (Negro)
Hopkins, Leonard
Hopkins, Thomas
Houston, John
Houston, Leonard
Houston, Robert
Hufington, Luke, Estate
Hufington, William, Jr.
Hufington, William, Sr.
Hurt, William
Hust, Cathewood
Hust, George
Hust, Joseph
Huston, Pariss
Hutson, Charles

James, Elias
James, Joshua
James, Ruben, Estate
Johnson, Edmond
Johnson, John
Johnson, William
Jones, Jacub
Jones, Nehemiah

Kershaw, Mitchell
Kilby, Daniel
King, Charles, store
King, Joseph, store
Kinney, William
Knoles, William

Lokey, Joseph
Lord, John

Magee, Samuel
Marlino, John
Mathis, Phillip
Mathis, Teaque, Estate
Melsen, William, Estate
Melson, Jesse
Melson, John
Melson, Joseph
Mesship, William
Messick, Covington
Messeck, John
Mitchell, Alexander
Mitchell, George, Esq., Land
Mitchell, Jesse
Mitchell, John
Mitchell, John, Major, Land
Mitchell, Thomas
Mittleton, James
Mittleton, William
Moore, Charles
Moore, Elsey
Moore, Ephraim
Moore, Gillis
Moore, Jesse
Moore, John
Moore, Littleton
Moore, Mathias
Moore, Thomas
Morgan, Elijah
Morrow, William

Night, Joshua

O'Neal, James
O'Neal, Thomas

O'Neal, William
Outten, Jesse
Outten, John

Parmore, Thomas
Pennawell, Solomon
Pepper, John, Jr.
Pepper, William
Permore, William
Pewsey, William
Polk, John, Land

Quillen, Joseph

Rigen, Isaac
Roach, Jaceb
Roach, Samuel
Roberson, Robert
Royel, Elijah

Safford, William
Sanders, Jesse
Sarogen, Phillip
Serogen, Samuel
Serogen, Thomas
Sharp, Hannah
Sharp, Joshua
Short, Elriah
Short, Isaac
Short, Isaac, s[on] of Sha[drac]k
Short, John, of Sha[drac]k
Short, Shadruck
Smiley, Robert, Land
Smith, Alexander
Smith, Andrew
Smith, Ezekiah
Smith, Henry
Smith, James
Smith, Thomas, Jr.
Smith, Thomas, Sr.
Spicer, Hales
Stokly, Jacob

Taylor, Ba[r]tho[lome]w
Timmons, Eli
Timmons, Ezekel
Timmons, John, Jr.
Timmons, John, Sr.
Timmons, Joshua
Timmons, Mathias
Timmons, Robert
Timmons, William
Tool, John
Truet, Thomas

Truit, James
Truit, Jarman
Truit, Josiah

Vaughan, Leven
Vaughan, William
Vinson, Benjamin
Vinson, George
Vinson, Solomon

Wallis, Thomas, Land
Weley, Joseph
Wells, Jesse

Wells, Thomas
Windsor, Joseph
Winget, Phillip
Winget, Smith
Wingit, Cannon
Winright, Isaac
Winright, John
Wootten, Jonathan
Workman, John
Workman, William
Wright, Jesse
Wright, Jesse, Jr.

LEWES AND REHOBOTH HUNDRED

Adams, John
Arnold, William
Art, Jacob, Estate

Bailey, Joseph
Bailey, Nathaniel, Estate
Bailey, William
Ball, Joshua
Barret, Humph[re]y
Bignal, John
Bignal, William
Bosoman, John
Brereton, William
Bruce, Alexander
Bryan, Jonathan
Burton, John

Caddy, John
Cameron, Andrew
Chambers, James
Chambers, John
Charles, Isaac
Charles, James
Coffin, William
Coleman, William
Conner, Daniel
Conolly, Francis
Coulter, Colbin
Coulter, Thomas
Coulter, William
Craig, Edward
Craig, John, Estate

Darby, Joseph
Davis, John
Dean, Caleb
Dood, Hebron
Dood, William
Drain, John
Dyer, Joseph

Edwards, Simon
Edwards, Simon, Jr.
Ennis, Levin
Ennis, Samuel
Ewin, Brinkley

Fisher, Harry
Fisher, Jabez
Fisher, Joshua
Fisher, Thomas
Fisher, William
Fleming, Archibald
Futcher, John

Gill, William
Gorden, Nathaniel
Gorden, Thomas
Green, Ambrose
Green, Richard

Hall, Adam
Hall, David, Estate
Hall, Joseph
Hall, Joshua
Hall, Simon
Hall, Thomas
Hall, William
Hall, William, smith
Harmonson, John
Harmonson, Peter
Hart, John
Hazzard, Artha
Hazzard, David
Hazzard, Uriah
Holland, Hannah
Holland, Isaac
Holland, William
Howard, Richard

Jackson, John
Jacobs, Albertus
Jacobs, Sarah
Jacobs, William
Jefferies, William
Jones, Penelope

Killen, Henry
Kollock, Hercules
Kollock, Jacob
Kollock, Margaret
Kollock, Phillips

Lamb, Abner
Lewes, Noble
Lewes, William
Lewis, Wrixam, Estate
Little, John
Little, Nickolas
Little, Richard

Marsh, John
Marsh, Peter
Marsh, Thomas
Marshall, Aaron
Marshall, John
Martin, Elisabeth
Martin, James
Martin, Josiah, Estate
Massey, Robert
Maull, John
Maull, William
McCracken, John
McHam, Evan
Miller, Josiah
Moore, Jacob
Morris, Levi
Murphy, Daniel

Neill, Harry
Newbold, James
Newbold, William
Newman, William
Nunez, Hannah

Oakey, Robert
Oakey, Saunders
Oakey, Thomas
Oliver, Charles
Orr, John

Parker, Anderson
Parker, George
Parker, Peter, Estate

Parker, William A.
Parsons, John
Paynter, Cornelius
Paynter, John
Paynter, Reece
Paynter, Samuel
Peters, Abigail
Prettyman, John
Prettyman, Sheppard
Pride, Luthy

Reccords, Levin
Reccords, Thomas
Rhoads, John, Estate
Roach, Levi
Roach, William
Rodney, John
Rowland, Samuel
Rowland, Thomas
Russell, John
Russell, Phillip

Shankland, David
Shankland, Rhoads
Shankland, Robert
Shields, Luke
Shields, Luke, Estate
Steel, John
Steel, William
Stevenson, David
Still, William
Stockley, Elisabeth
Stockley, Jacob
Stockley, William

Thompson, James
Thompson, Samuel
Thompson, William
Train, David
Treglohan, Philip
Turner, Isaac
Turner, John

Vent, James
Virden, Marnix

Walker, George
Walker, Jacob
Walker, Thomas
Wave, William, Land
West, Thomas
West, William
Westley, John, Estate
White, Isaac, Estate
White, John

White, Newcomb
White, Paul
White, Peter
White, Robert
White, William
White, William, son of Jacob
White, Wrixham
White, Wrixham, Estate
Wiles, Robert
Wilson, Thomas

Wiltbank, Cornelius
Wiltbank, George
Wiltbank, John, Esq.
Woolf, John
Woolf, Jonathan
Woolf, Reece, Jr.
Woolf, Reece, Sr.
Wright, Peter F.
Wright, Thomas
Wyatt, Sacker

NANTICOKE HUNDRED

Adams, George
Adams, Isaac
Adams, Jacob
Adams, John
Adams, William
Aile, David
Anderson, William
Argoe, Alexander

Bayley, Bagwell
Boice, Benjamin
Boice, John
Boice, Joshua
Boice, Prittyman
Bounds, Mattilda
Bozman, Daniel

Callahan, Dennis
Carlile, John
Carlile, William
Carlile, Zachariah
Carpenter, Messick
Cavender, David
Cavender, Henry
Collins, John
Conway, Jacob
Conway, John, of John
Conway, John, of Levin
Conway, John, of Philip
Conway, Levin
Conway, Philip
Coverdal, Elias
Coverdal, Israel
Coverdal, Jacob
Coverdal, Levin
Coverdal, Matthew
Coverdal, Matthew, Jr.
Coverdal, Prichard, of T.
Crankfield, Purnal
Crocket, Elizabeth
Croket, Winder
Coverdale, Charles
Coverdale, Luke

Danohoe, Truet
Dawson, Jonathan
Deep Creek Furnace Company
Depray, Selba
Donohoe, Major
Durham, Richard

Ecliot, John
Evans, Calab
Evans, Elisha
Evans, Jehu
Evans, Owen

Farman, Prichard
Fisher, Curtis
Fisher, George Har[dy]
Fisher, Isaac
Fisher, John
Fisher, John, of Hardy
Fleetwood, Luke
Fleetwood, Nehemiah
Fleetwood, William
Fowlar, Arthur
Fowler, Asa
Fowlar, Jesse

Griffeth, Avery
Griffeth, Charles
Griffeth, John, Jr.
Griffeth, Joseph
Griffeth, Joseph, Jr.
Griffeth, Moses
Griffeth, Salathiel
Griffeth, Samuel

Harris, John
Harris, Robert
Harris, Zachariah
Hart, Robert
Hays, Nathaniel
Hemmons, John
Hinds, Daniel
Hinds, Nathaniel

Hinson, John
Holt, John
Hurley, Caleb
Hurley, Edmond
Hurley, Pharoah
Hust, William

Ingram, Isaac
Ingram, Thomas

Jackson, Peter
Johnson, Christion, of Eli
Johnson, Elisha
Johnson, Jacob
Johnson, John, of W[illia]m
Johnson, Joseph
Jones, James
Jones, William

Knox, Charles
Knox, Daniel
Knox, James
Knox, Thomas

Lain, John
Lain, John, Jr.
Lambdon, Robert
Lard, Thomas
Lavety, Mary, (widow)
Laws, Allecander (Deceased), Land
Laws, Elijah
Laws, John
Laws, Lowdorwick
Laws, Saxty [Saxe Gotha], Estate
Layton, Elijah
Layton, Solomon
Lecat, Elijah
Lewes, Stephen, Land
Linch, Abram, Sr.
Linch, Abram, of Jon[athan]
Linch, John
Lindal, Josep
Long, Daniel
Lowry, James

Martin, David
Martin, John
Marvel, Philip
Marvel, Thomas
Massey, Mary
Massey, Moses
McCauley, Eli
McCauley, John
McCauley, Robert
Morgan, Bradbery
Morgan, Matthew

Mosely, John
Muirs, James, Land
Mullinex, John
Murphy, Jesse
Murphy, Joseph

O'Day, John
O'Day, Owen
Outten, Abram
Outten, O'Bed
Owens, David
Owens, John
Owens, Jonathan
Owens, Robert
Owens, William

Parker, Eli
Passwaters, Isaac
Passwaters, Jonas
Paswaters, Prichard, Sr.
Paswaters, William
Paswaters, Prichard
Phips, Absalom
Polk, Charles, Esq.
Polk, John, of John
Polk, John, of Josh[ua]
Polk, Joseph, of Jos[eph]
Polk, Joshua
Polk, Joshua, Estate
Pollock, James
Pricliff, William

Ricliff, Charles
Ricliff, Reuben
Right, Joy
Rilley, Joseph

Sammons, Benjamin
Sammons, Job
Sammons, Saul
Samuels, Hance
Samuels, Peter
Samuels, William
Sharp, John
Short, Abraham
Short, Abram, of Eli
Short, Adam
Short, Adam, of Dan[iel]
Short, Dennard
Short, Eli
Short, John
Short, John, Jr.
Short, Purnal
Short, Tilghman
Smith, James
Smith, Joseph

Smith, Peter
Smith, Stephen
Smith, Stouton
Smith, William
Spicer, Elsy
Spicer, Philip
Staton, Jehu
Swain, John
Swain, William

Tatman, Joshua
Tatman, Nehemiah
Tatman, Purnal
Tatman, William
Taylor, Stephen
Tindle, Charles
Tindle, Purnal
Tindle, Samuel
Tirner, William (Deceased)
Truet, Samuel
Truet, Tatman
Truet, Thomas
Truet, William

Veach, Thomas
Veach, Zadock

Walker, William
Waller, Nathaniel
Warren, Cloudsbrough
Web, Benjamin, Jr.
White, Smith
Willen, Charles
Willen, Thomas
Willey, Absalom
Willey, Absolom
Willey, Edmond
Willey, James
Willey, John
Willey, Mary
Willey, Robert
Williams, Charles
Williams, Henry
Williams, John
Williss, John
Winsor, Jesse, Estate

NORTH WEST FORK HUNDRED

Adams, Absolem
Adams, Batt
Adams, Daniel
Adams, Elijah
Adams, Enals
Adams, George
Adams, James, Sr.
Adams, James, of Absolom
Adams, Jeremiah
Adams, John
Adams, Nathan
Adams, Roger
Adams, Thomas Nutter
Adams, William
Anderson, James
Anderson, Major
Armit, Jonathan
Arnett, Ruffus
Axwell, John

Badley, William
Baker, Riley
Baker, William
Banard, John, Land
Barton, James
Bayly, Clement
Bayley, John Lee
Baynard, John
Bennett, Samuel
Blocksum, John

Bosman, Risden
Bowness, William
Bradley, Isaac, Esq.
Bradley, Joseph
Bready, Solomon
Brown, Anderton, Jr.
Brown, Anderton, Sr.
Brown. Charles. of Cannon
Brown, Charles, of Charles
Brown, Charles, of John
Brown, Charles, of Joseph
Brown, Clement
Brown, Curtis
Brown, Edward
Brown, Ezekiel
Brown, Francis
Brown, Humphryes
Brown, James, Jr.
Brown, James, Sr.
Brown, Jessy, Land
Brown, John
Brown, John (Mashahope)
  [Marshy Hope]
Brown, John, merchant
Brown, Thomas
Brown, White
Buchanan, Sarah, (widow)
Butler, William
Byas, Standley

Callison, John
Camplin, Henry
Cannon, Abram
Cannon, Absolem
Cannon, Charles
Cannon, Clarkson
Cannon, Edward
Cannon, Elisha
Cannon, Elizabeth, (widow)
Cannon, Hayward
Cannon, Hudson
Cannon, Hughet
Cannon, Isaac
Cannon, Isaac, son of Absolom
Cannon, Isaac, son of Jacob
Cannon, Jacob
Cannon, Jeremiah
Cannon, Jessey
Cannon, John
Cannon, Joseph
Cannon, Leven, Estate
Cannon, Levi
Cannon, Mary, (widow of W[illia]m)
Cannon, Neubell
Cannon, Newton
Cannon, Nutter
Cannon, Richard
Cannon, Robert
Cannon, Stephen
Cannon, Stephen, Jr.
Cannon, Whitinton
Cannon, William
Cannon, William, son of Leven
Cannon, William Nutter
Cannon, Willis
Carpenter, Sarah, (widow)
Carrell, Clement
Causay, William
Chipman, Draper
Clarkson, Joseph
Clarkson, Robert
Clarkson, Thomas
Clarkson, William
Clarkson, W[illia]m, Estate
Clifton, Betsey, (widow)
Clifton, Jonathan, widow
Cliffton, Henry
Cliffton, Leven, Estate
Cliffton, Robert
Coats, Thomas Peach
Collins, John
Collins, Thomas
Cope, Jonathan
Corbin, Stephen
Coulburn, Catharine
Coulburn, Elijah

Coulburn, Joseph
Coulburn, Michael
Coulburn, Thomas
Coulburns, Stephen, Estate
Curryir, Thomas

Darters, Hudson
Darters, James
Dawson, Edward
Dawson, Joseph
Dill, Fredrick
Dill, Philip
Downs, Abram
Downs, Asy
Downs, Ezekiel
Downs, Henry, (widower)
Dukes, Isaac
Dukes, Isaac, Jr.
Elbert, Samuel
Eliat, John
Elliots, John, Land
Ely, Abner
Ervin, William
Evans, William

Finch, William
Fitzgerrald, George
Flowers, Henry
Flowers, Jeremiah
Flowers, John
Flowers, Samuel
Flowers, Tho[ma]s, Estate
Forman, Joseph, Land

Gauslin, Samuel
Gauslin, Waitman
Gauslin, Waitman, Jr.
Graham, John
Green, John
Grey, Joseph
Grey, Thomas, schoolmaster
Grey, Thomas, shoemaker
Grey, William
Griffin, James
Griffith, Jessey
Griffith, Robert, Land
Griffith, Seth
Gullet, Joshua

Handy, John
Handy, John, farmer
Handy, John, joiner
Handy, Samuel
Hardy, Smart
Harper, William, (widower)
Harris, James, Land

Hasty, Nemiah
Hatfield, Jonathan
Hemis, Perry
Henols, Thomas
Hickman, Nicholas
Higman, Curtis
Higman, James
Higman, Leven
Higman, Nathan
Higman, Nicholas
Higman, Priscella
Higman, Robert
Higman, Thomas
Hitch, Gilles
Hitch, Mary, (widow)
Hitch, Spencer
Hitch, Whitinton
Hitch, William
Hollis, Hinson
Hooper, Henry
Hooper, Henry, of Thomas
Hooper, John
Hooper, Thomas
Horsey, Nathan, heirs
Hubbert, John
Hughs, Phillip
Hurst, William
Hurt, Daniel
Hutchison, John

Jackson, Augustus
Jackson, Jeremiah Rust
Jackson, Julia Augustus
Jacobs, Constantine
Jacobs, Curtis
Jacobs, William
Jessup, William
Jester, Samuel
Johnston, Jonathan
Jones, Isaac
Jones, John
Jones, John, of Gauslin
Jones, Thomas, blacksmith
Jones, Zadock
Juitt, Robert
Jump, Oliver
Jump, Sophia, (widow)
Jump, William

Kellins, Abel, Land
Kendal, Jacob
King, Henry

Laws, Alexander, Land
Laws, John, merchant
Laws, Thomas

Layton, Burton, Land
Layton, David
Layton, Elijah
Layton, Hughet
Layton, James
Layton, Louder
Layton, Nemiah
Layton, Purnal
Layton, Shadrach, Land
Layton, Spencer
Layton, Thomas
Layton, Tilghman
Layton, William
Lecatt, Joseph
Ledanham, . . . , (widow of John)
Ledenham, Ebenezar
Ledenham, Thomas
Lewis, Leven
Libbey, Catrap
Libby, Richard
Lister, Nicholas
Littleton, Charles
Lowery, James, Land

Manship, Henry
Marim, Sarah
Marine, Charles
Mastin, Gilly
Mastin, John
Means, Henry
Means, Ikybud [Ichabod]
Melony, William
Merrale, William
Milliken, Thomas
Mills, Cannon
Mills, John
Millvin, Isaac
Minner, Elisha
Minnor, Edward
Minnor, Richard
Montgomery, William, Land
Morgan, George
Morgan, Jonathan
Morris, Curtis
Morris, Daniel
Morris, Ezekia
Morris, Henry
Morris, John
Morris, John, of Daniel
Morris, Masten
Morris, Nathaniel
Murphy, Joseph, Jr.

Neale, Arthur
Neale, John
Neale, Joseph

Neale, William
Needham, Michel
Netter, David
Nicolls, James
Nicolls, Joseph
Nicolls, Leven
Nicolls, Nemiah
Nicolls, William
Noble, William
Norman, John, Jr.
Norman, John, Sr.
Nutter, Caleb
Nutter, Nancey, (widow)
Nutter, Thomas

Obear, Joshua
Otwell, Triffiniah
Outabridge, Stephen
Owens, David, Estate
Owens, Sarah, Estate

Palston, John
Pavey, Samuel
Penny, Asy
Poet, William
Polk, Clement, Land
Polk, Daniel, Esq.
Polk, David
Polk, John, son of Joseph, Land
Polk, Trustin Laws
Polk, William
Price, William
Prider, James
Pullet, John
Pullet, Jonathan

Quinaly, William

Read, Isaac
Records, . . ., (widow of Henry)
Records, Charles
Records, Joseph
Records, Leven
Records, Loxly
Records, William
Richards, David
Robinson, John, blacksmith
Robinson, John, farmer
Robinson, Ralph
Rodgers, Christopher
Rodgers, Clement
Ross, Anthony
Ross, Charles
Ross, Leven
Ross, Mathew
Ross, Robert, Jr.

Ross, Robert, Sr.
Ross, Thomas
Ross, William, Jr.
Ross, William, Sr.
Ross, Zaddock
Rotton, Thomas
Rotton, Zebulon
Russell, John
Rust, John, Land
Rust, Peter

Saughterfield, Herman
Scovymount, Fardinand
Sewett, John
Shebe, Daniel
Shenehan, Clifferd
Short, Adam
Smith, Allan
Smith, Charles
Smith, Charles, (Adams)
Smith, Curtis
Smith, Ezekiel
Smith, George
Smith, Henry
Smith, Henry, of George
Smith, James
Smith, James, Jr.
Smith, Jesse
Smith, Job
Smith, Mathew
Smith, Obediah
Smith, Robert
Smith, William
Smith, William, of Gibson
Smith, William, of Maryland
Snow, Obed
Spence, Alexander
Spence, Henry
Spence, James
Spence, James, Jr.
Spencer, . . ., (widow of Joh
Stack, Joseph
Stafford, Levy
Stafford, Thomas
Stayton, William, Land
Steel, Henry, Land
Stephens, John, wheelwright
Sterling, Josiah
Storrey, Frances
Swiget, Henry

Tennant, John
Thorn, Sydenham, Land
Tod, Stephen
Traves, Henry
Tull, Abel

Tull, Andrew
Tull, Chambers
Tull, Elijah
Tull, Ephraim
Tull, James
Tull, Jesse, of Jesse
Tull, Jesse, of Joshua
Tull, John
Tull, Leven
Tull, Richard
Tull, Whitinton
Turner, Sidney, (widow)
Turpin, Francies
Turpin, Ja[me]s, heirs
Twyford, Bartholomew
Twyford, Charles
Twyford, John, Land
Twyford, Solomon

Wallace, Henry, Estate
Wallace, William
Wallers, Nathaniel, Land
Watts, Elijah
Watts, George
Watts, John
Wheatly, John

White, Edward, Esq.
White, William, Land
Williams, Charles
Williams, Elzey
Williams, Leven
Williams, Morgain
Williams, Morgan, of David
Williams, Robert
Williams, Spencer
Williams, Thomas
Williams, Whitinton
Wilson, . . ., (widow of William)
Wilson, John
Wilson, Samuel, Land
Wilson, William, Estate
Windror, Cord
Wingate, Andrew
Wood, Jno., Estate
Wood, Stephen
Woodgates, . . ., Estate
Wright, Edward, Land
Wright, James, Land
Wright, Jesse, of Leven
Wright, Joshua
Wright, Francies

FINIS

MAP
of the State of
Delaware
and Eastern Shore of
MARYLAND
With the Soundings of the Bay of Delaware
From actual survey & soundings made in
1799. 1800. & 1801 by the Author.